W9-ACC-885

Home Run

Home Run

LEARN GOD'S GAME PLAN FOR LIFE AND LEADERSHIP

KEVIN MYERS
AND
JOHN C. MAXWELL

FOREWORD BY CRAIG GROESCHEL

NEW YORK BOSTON NASHVILLE

12Stone® Church is a registered trademark.

Kevin Myers and John C. Maxwell are represented by Yates & Yates,
www.yates2.com.

All scripture quotations, unless otherwise indicated, are taken from the Holy
Bible, New International Version®, NIV®. Copyright ©1973, 1978, 1984, 2011
by Biblica, Inc.™ Used by permission of Zondervan. All rights reserved
worldwide. www.zondervan.com The "NIV" and "New International Version"
are trademarks registered in the United States Patent and Trademark Office by
Biblica, Inc.™

FaithWords
Hachette Book Group
237 Park Avenue
New York, NY 10017

faithwords.com

Printed in the United States of America

RRD-C

First Edition: February 2014
10 9 8 7 6 5 4 3 2 1

FaithWords is a division of Hachette Book Group, Inc.
The FaithWords name and logo are trademarks of
Hachette Book Group, Inc.

The publisher is not responsible for websites (or their content) that are not
owned by the publisher.

Library of Congress Cataloging-in-Publication Data has been applied for.

ISBN 978-1-4555-7722-4 (hardcover)

This book is dedicated to the people of 12Stone Church...

Thank you for inspiring the development of Home Run *more than a decade ago. You are making a huge impact at your "post." Eternity will affirm we had the best of times reaching the lost, serving the least, and raising up leaders.*
You are Mighty Warriors!

—KEVIN MYERS (AKA PK)

Thank you for partnering in the creation of the John C. Maxwell Leadership Center. Together we are changing lives nationally and globally.

—JOHN C. MAXWELL

Free information, stories, videos, small group material, and church resources are available at www.HomeRunLife.com.

Contents

Foreword

by Craig Groeschel, Founder and Senior Pastor, LifeChurch.tv

Do you know someone who seems like an overnight success story? Whatever they touch turns to gold. Everything seems to come easily for them.

Then there are the rest of us.

Success doesn't come easily for us. It seems we are striking out more than we are getting on base. We long for a better life. To make a difference. But days turn into weeks, then months, then years. And the dreams we once had seem to fade into the distance.

We wonder about ourselves. The questions we ask turn personal. *What am I doing wrong?*

If you've ever felt discouraged, worn out, or let down, I've got great news for you. You are holding the right book in your hand.

What you are about to read could be the best and most helpful book you have read in a long time. Because while a rare group of people seem to live with instant success and significance, the vast majority of us don't.

Keep this in mind: just because you don't have the rags-to-riches story, doesn't mean God doesn't have an amazing plan for your life. But I also believe He wants to do something in you before He does more through you.

And that's where Kevin Myers comes in.

This book is long overdue. The first time I heard Kevin's story, I told him, "You have to put your story into a book!"

Being modest, he shrugged off my suggestion and tried to change the subject.

I was too passionate to be polite and talked over him, "Listen to me! You don't understand. People need to hear this story. Pastors need it. Business leaders need it. Parents need it. Teenagers need it." Then I told him again as plainly as I could, "You...have...to...put...your...story...into...a...book."

I'm a big believer in the message of this book for several reasons. First, Kevin is not an overnight success story. In fact, his story is quite the opposite. After starting a church, his congregation didn't grow to more than 200 people in the first seven years. In the "church world," that means his church would not likely ever see over 200 people in attendance. But Kevin was persistent and faithful to God's call. Then something amazing happened. Not only did his church surpass 200, but it went on to reach 700, 1,800, 5,000, 10,000, 15,000—and it is still growing! After years of living what seemed to be a dead-end dream, now Kevin leads one of the largest churches in America.

His story is both inspirational and bottom-shelf practical. Kevin has a unique ability to simultaneously encourage and instruct. He will show you four very specific and helpful keys to succeeding at what matters most.

Finally, I am a Kevin Myers fan. He is humble, teachable, wise, and full of integrity. He combines a deep love for God and a rich understanding of leadership that will walk you through a step-by-step journey of becoming all God wants you to be.

Get ready to round the bases.

With God's help and through this book, it's time to hit a home run!

We want to say thank you to

Charlie Wetzel, our writer, who worked on this project
for five years

Stephanie Wetzel, who read and edited the early manuscript
in its various versions

Linda Eggers, John's executive assistant

Diane Heller, Kevin's executive assistant

Home Run

1

The Life You Want

Introduction by John C. Maxwell

Are you living the life that you want—life to the full, as Jesus described in John 10:10? I believe every follower of Christ has the potential to do that. Yet too often believers' lives don't look much different from those of people who don't follow God. Heartbreakingly, research shows that most believers live no better and no differently than non-believers. For example, believers don't seem to handle money any better than non-believers. According to John W. Kennedy writing in *Christianity Today*, "There is little difference between the amounts that Christians and non-Christians earn, spend, save, charge, or donate to charities."[1] Believers seem to struggle with pornography and lust just as much as non-believers.[2] And according to researcher George Barna, divorce rates for Christians and non-Christians are virtually identical at 32 and 33 percent.[3] Why is that?

I believe that many Christians are missing some foundational principles and practices of the faith. Many of these were taught to my generation when we were children. And they were definitely embraced and embodied by the generation of my parents. God wants to change us from the inside out. Many people try to grow from the outside in. The bad news is that it just doesn't work. The good news is that this book can help a person to change and grow the right way, and to learn those missing pieces of faith and life development.

A Life with Great Potential

Kevin Myers has discovered a new hook for biblical truths that are as old as the Old Testament. In the pages of Scripture and through his own life experience, he has found a pattern for living that God uses to help His people do life well. It also helps them to make good decisions, to grow, and to lead.

As a communicator, I appreciate a great "hook," a fresh and effective way of teaching something. Before I get into the great hook Kevin discovered to teach these truths, let me first tell you about him. I've known Kevin since he was seventeen years old, and he came to a leadership conference where I was speaking. As a kid in Bible college, he was sharp, a little bit brash, and determined to do great things for God.

Our paths crossed several times during the next few years. I remember when he introduced me to his wife, Marcia, soon after they were married. Trust me—the boy married way above himself. Because Kevin was in the same denomination and because he worked for my friend Wayne Schmidt in Grand Rapids, Michigan, early in his career I was aware of him. In fact, when I learned that Kevin and Marcia planned to plant a church in North Metro Atlanta in the late '80s, Margaret and I wrote a check for $500 to show our support.

The marking moment in Kevin's and my relationship came at a leadership conference I hosted several years after Kevin planted his church, 12Stone. I'll let him tell you that story. But let me say this: Kevin is one of the finest communicators I know in the United States. He's become a dear friend to me and to EQUIP, my international non-profit leadership training organization. I have gotten the opportunity to mentor him for more than a decade. And I feel that more than anyone else, he has taken the baton of church leadership that I passed after I left full-time pastoral leadership in the local church, and he has run with it. He is leading the kind of church that I would have liked to lead, had God allowed me to stay in pastoral ministry in the local church.

Kevin is highly energetic, creative, and passionate. He's a good leader, a good thinker, and a lifelong student of leadership. He is a great father and husband. And one of his favorite things is riding his Harley-Davidson motorcycle. His leadership style may be somewhat different from mine, but his heart for people and passion for sharing Christ are the same. He has become a dear friend.

Timeless Truths in a Timely Package

Kevin has been teaching the ideas in this book for nearly fifteen years. The concept is rooted in Romans 12:1–2:

> Therefore, I urge you, brothers and sisters, in view of God's mercy, to offer your bodies as a living sacrifice, holy and pleasing to God—this is your true and proper worship. Do not conform to the pattern of this world, but be transformed by the renewing of your mind. Then you will be able to test and approve what God's will is—his good, pleasing and perfect will.

The core idea is that there is a pattern the world follows for living, and there is a different pattern that God desires us to follow that enables people to live life to the full. And the hook that Kevin uses to teach it is baseball.

I've been aware of this teaching of Kevin's for over a decade, and I've been encouraging him to share it with others for years. True to Kevin's personality, he wanted to thoroughly road-test it first. He wanted to make sure it really helped people and could stand the test of time before sharing it more broadly outside his own church. He also wanted to build personal credibility in his leadership before authoring his first book. In the early years, his church struggled—much more than I was ever aware of. It humbled him, and it taught him many of the lessons he's learned.

Today 12Stone Church averages more than thirteen thousand people every weekend at four campuses. In 2010, it was the fastest-growing church in the United States according to *Outreach* magazine.[4] And the church is still growing and working toward opening additional campuses. It is making a difference in its community of Gwinnett County, Georgia, an area of a million people. Kevin is determined to reach as many people as possible for as long as God allows him to serve.

The church is also working toward equipping leaders and helping other churches. For instance, 12Stone has a residency program for young pastors just starting out in their careers. And it is in the process of opening a leadership center. In fact, by the time you're reading this book, the leadership center will be built and helping to equip leaders for the advancement of God's Kingdom. You'll learn more about that later in the book.

When Kevin told me he was finally ready to share these ideas, I was determined to help him. That's when I offered to co-author the book with him. I want everyone to whom I've taught leadership over the years to benefit from the ideas in this book. If you want to live God's way and you want to have a rock-solid foundation upon which to build your leadership, you need these lessons.

When Kevin originally taught these concepts to his church, he called it "Diamond Life." But as we talked about it, I told him that what he was really describing was how to have a home run life. And that's when we decided to name this book *Home Run*. Everyone wants to score in life. Everyone wants to be a winner. This book will show you how.

This book contains Kevin's story and the lessons God has taught him over the years. It's a story of success, yet Kevin shares not only the good, but also the bad and the ugly. Along the way, I will weigh in and give you my perspective. I'll also provide application and discussion questions at the end of each chapter that will help you to process what you learn and incorporate it into your life.

God has a dream for your life. He loves you. He made you uniquely. He has given you gifts and talents. He created you with a purpose. And you can fulfill it! You can learn to be content, as the Apostle Paul did. You can live life to the full, as Jesus offered. It means following God and doing things His way. But always remember that God ultimately wants the best for you. When we do things God's way, the journey isn't always what we expect, but it's always better than we imagined and more than we deserve. Let's turn the page and get started.

2

Hopes, Dreams, and Delays

Everyone has dreams. They start when we daydream as kids, with boys often imitating Superman and girls playing Superstar Barbie. But soon enough we form real dreams for our future. We dream of having success in a career. Having great friends. Possessing the freedom to travel and seek adventure. Finding the love of our life and saying "I do" for keeps. Then adding some kids. Getting a house and going on the Disney vacation. (I dreamed of having five kids. After the reality of one I was happy to stop at two, but that didn't work. I now have four. I love them all, but that's another story.)

Whether we ever thought about it or not, we also hoped that when we looked in the mirror, we respected the person we saw there. And even if we didn't use these exact words, we wanted our life to matter— to make a difference, to have meaning, to count. We dreamed of having a good life, a full life. We wanted to "hit a home run."

Think about when you were young, maybe when you were getting out of high school or on your way to college. What was your dream? Career success? Financial success? Married and in love for life? A solid family with kids? Trusted friends? Free time? Freedom from addiction? Soul peace? Spiritually resolved faith? Health? Happiness?

Don't rush past this question. Many people have long since quit on their life dreams because of deep disappointment. I hope that doesn't describe you. A life without hopes and dreams is no life at all.

The name of this book is *Home Run*. Most of us want to experience the equivalent of a home run in life, a life where the dreams of our youth are fulfilled. Do you have that kind of life? Have you succeeded? Or are you more like me, someone who has experienced a whole lot of unfulfilled hopes and broken dreams?

Or maybe you've done well in one area of life, but struck out in another. Many win the race in their career, but crash their marriage. They get their finances stable, but make their family unstable. They build up their reputation for success, but break down their body in the process. They drive toward a goal they create, yet drift farther from the God who created them.

Dreaming about a great life is a lot easier than building one, isn't it? Those of us who win in one area and fail in another wonder, *Is there a way to get a home run in all areas of life? Is there some secret that may have eluded me on the journey of life?* I often had these thoughts as my hopes and dreams were crashing.

There Is More for Us

I believe that God has more for us than most of us are living. He wants us to live a life that matters—a home run kind of life. Why do I say that? Because Jesus said, "I have come that they may have life, and have it to the full."[1] Jesus coming to earth was without a doubt the most profound moment in all of human history. The God of the universe lived in human flesh in the midst of our broken dreams. The very fact of that should tell us four things:

1. God Loves Us *More* than We Will Ever Know

It's very difficult for us to wrap our heads around God's love for us. To paraphrase Jesus when He was trying to express how deeply God cares for us, He said, "God so loved this world that he gave me, his one and only son. He did this so that whoever believes in me would not perish but have everlasting life."[2]

That can be hard to believe in a world of broken dreams and broken families. After my parents went through a divorce when I was eleven and twelve years old, my father became indifferent toward me. I can tell you that the teen years are a rough season to experience distance from your dad. That was no small thing for me to get through or get over. And in subsequent years, I was at great risk of projecting the image of my earthly father onto my Heavenly Father. But deep down, I knew that God is not indifferent toward us.

Life to the full as Jesus described begins with knowing that God loves us more than we will ever know. No matter how little or how much you believe in God's love, there's more. Even if you are the most secure person in the world who knows to the depths of your soul that God loves you, you still haven't scratched the surface of God's love.

2. There Is *More* to God

No matter how close you are to God and how well you know Him, you need to remember that there is more to God. The depth and breadth of the power of God's greatness has never been measured. The more you know God, the more you discover there is to know about Him. The closer you get to Him, the bigger He gets. Even when you get to the end of yourself, you are never at the end of God. Pursue God and in time you will join the ancient writers who simply confess, "God has no equal in heaven or on earth."

3. God Has Put *More* in Us

God created us in His image and in His likeness from the beginning. He created us to rule on His behalf over the earth. And He would have us know that He has put more talent in each of us than we have ever trained. That's why you can spend a lifetime growing and never be done. We were, in fact, created for the adventure of growing for a lifetime.

God has also put more tenacity in each of us than we have ever tapped. The only reason anything is truly over for us is that we choose to quit, not because we have to quit. God has put a strong will into human beings. And when we choose to trust Jesus for the forgiveness of sin and to follow His game plan for life, God puts even more in us— His Holy Spirit literally indwells us. That gives us the power of God in us so that we can pursue the dreams God has for us.

4. God Has *More* for Us

Early one morning I was reading the story of David, and I was struck by something I read. It forever reshaped my thinking about God. David's story is familiar to us, and he is known for many things: For his battle with Goliath when he was a teenager. For being a shepherd who become a great warrior and then the king of Israel. For writing the Psalms. But we also know about his failure because of his affair with Bathsheba. This particular morning, I discovered I had been so focused on David's failure and broken dream that I missed the nature of God revealed in the story.

After the affair, God used Nathan the prophet to confront David's sin. Speaking for God, Nathan said, "I gave your master's house to you…I gave you all Israel and Judah. And if all this had been too little, I would have given you even *more*."[3] As I read this verse, God arrested my attention. God wanted more for David. And I sensed that

God was trying to make me understand that He wants more for all those He loves.

It transformed how I saw God, and I have never been the same. The experience reset in me the truth of who God is by nature. He is a generous God who desires to give us more. No wonder the early church was encouraged by the words in Ephesians describing God as one "who is able to do immeasurably more than all we ask or imagine."[4]

John's Perspective

Kevin references one of my favorite verses when he quotes Ephesians 3:20. Too many people underestimate the desire of God to bless them out of His love. We should never have a scarcity mind-set when it comes to God. He is the Author of everything, the Creator who formed the universe out of nothing. His resources and His love can never run out. And because He has told us that He loves us, we should have an abundance mind-set. God wants more for you. The question is whether you are willing to receive it.

God is intimately and personally involved in the dreams of our lives. And what does He want for us? More. By that, I don't mean more material things. I mean more on a deeper level: more significance, more good relationships, more soul satisfaction, more impact, more connection with God—life to the full. So if Jesus came that we might have life to the full, how come most of us seem to live half full or even empty? The answer is simple but also supernatural. If you're willing to continue with us on the journey of this book, we offer a game plan for life and leadership that leads to a full life. The journey begins with a bus ride.

Take the Bus Ride

"How did you get John Maxwell to personally mentor you?" I've been asked that question repeatedly. My answer? I took a bus ride.

In January 1997, fifty leaders from 12Stone Church loaded onto a charter bus bound for Winston-Salem, North Carolina. All these volunteer leaders had to take off work and pay their own way. The destination? A John Maxwell Leadership Conference.

The previous fall, I had experienced an unmistakable God prompt. I've had many over the years, but never one to attend a leadership conference. And this prompt had several things working against it. The conference was a five-hour bus ride away. It was also at a bad time: Who would want to do this right after the Christmas and New Year holidays?

I hesitated for a couple of weeks, almost dismissing the prompt as the result of indigestion. But the press in my spirit was undeniable, so I blocked out the time on my calendar. Then I asked fifty or so 12Stone leaders to join me, awkwardly trying to explain the invitation: "Um, well, God told me to attend this conference and invite you. He'll have to tell you the same thing, because it's quite inconvenient just after the holidays." Curiously, we filled the bus.

Though I'd met John when I was seventeen, attended several conferences over the years, and read every book he wrote, I was not sure he'd remember me. So before the event, I dropped him a note to say, "Fifty people are coming from our church and I hope it's a good conference!"

It was a long bus ride to Winston-Salem, and when we arrived late in the evening at our hotel, we discovered that they had lost our reservations. Fortunately, we had the confirmation number; unfortunately they had no rooms. So the hotel staff scrambled and found us rooms at a better hotel at their expense. It was a hassle, but we made the best of it.

As we were all checking into our rooms at the new hotel, the buzz began. "Look," somebody said, "there's John Maxwell." He was checking in. We had been moved to his hotel. I shook his hand and tried to appear self-confident, though I actually felt intimidated. I felt foolish for writing the note to him, but at least I had connected with the man who fueled my leadership engine.

The next morning as we loaded up the bus, we saw that the guy who was supposed to drive John over to the conference had locked his keys in the car with the engine running. So we invited John onto the bus to get a ride to his own conference. We dished out the sarcasm, and John had no trouble returning it. It was a fun ride, and it set the tone for an engaging conference for us. As a gesture of generous thanks, John bought lunch for all fifty of us. And at the close of the conference, John agreed to join us for dinner—something I later understood never happens.

All through the meal, I sat at the table with *the* John Maxwell experiencing two colliding emotions: excitement and terror. I was excited because I could finally ask the leadership guru anything I wanted. The terror: What on earth do I ask the leadership guru without looking stupid? Fortunately, the excitement won out and I asked, "John, what would you do if you were facing a major conflict with your denominational leaders and felt like you needed to walk away? Literally and legally separate?"

John and I were both in the Wesleyan denomination, so he understood the complications and the nuances of my question. I explained some details, and he offered, "Kevin, sometimes God will put a less gifted leader over a more gifted leader to test the humility of the rising leader. You have to decide if it's time to leave or time to humble yourself."

If God Himself had chosen to speak audibly, it could not have been more cutting or clear. In that moment, I understood that it's possible for leaders to be *right* in their position and simultaneously *wrong* in their actions. I knew I would have to go humble myself. (How that played out is a long story for another time. However, know that 12Stone is still gratefully linked to our denomination while having the freedom to lead with our unique calling in the community.)

The dinner came to an end, and it seemed good to close with a prayer. For no particular reason, I asked all fifty people to form a circle in the private room we occupied. We thanked John for coming, and I asked then board member and friend Chris Huff to pray.

What happened next would take the Holy Spirit to explain. All I know is that I was spiritually overwhelmed without specific cause or reason. As Chris prayed, I began tearing up, which caught me off guard. I felt foolish—until I opened my eyes and discovered others were also weeping, including John.

"Kevin," John said, turning to me, "I think the Holy Spirit just asked me to mentor you. If you're interested, that is my offer."

I was undone. It took everything in me to hold it together emotionally. I know this sounds wimpy, but I was unable to regain my composure. And nobody but God and me—not John Maxwell, not my closest friends, not even my wife—knew why. It signified a life-changing spiritual shift, which I will explain in the next chapter.

We left that evening for the long bus ride home. Those five hours became a rolling church service of God's grace. Person after person took the mike and spoke about what God had stirred in them during the conference or after the prayer moment.

That remains one of the ten most supernaturally charged moments in my life. And to think, I could have missed it had I dismissed the prompt from God that I'd experienced weeks before. How many times has God whispered something in our spirit that we casually dismissed? Sometimes a prompt can be as unusual as a bus ride. It can be a simple act of kindness. God may ask us to start something. Or stop something. Or risk something. What would my life be like today if I had been a no-show for that leadership conference? I would have missed out on having John as a mentor! We need to be God's "Yes Man" or

"Yes Woman" every time God speaks. The *more* that God has for us is usually on the other side of "Yes, Lord."

John's Perspective

That was the only time the person who was supposed to drive me to a conference to speak locked his keys in the car with the engine running. I should have known God was up to something. When Kevin's friend Chris prayed, I *knew* God was up to something because His presence was *clear.* I followed God's leading by asking Kevin if I could mentor him. I have been rewarded greatly by watching Kevin grow in his leadership. Mentoring him has been a joy because he always prepares before we meet, asks hard questions, and implements what he learns. And he does it all for the glory of God.

If you sense that God is prompting you to do something, don't discount or dismiss it. Follow God's lead. You never know where He may be leading you.

So the short answer to how I got John Maxwell to mentor me is that I obeyed a God prompt. To understand the importance of his offer, I'll need to take you farther back in my personal history.

God Gives All of Us Dreams

When we went on the bus trip in 1997, 12Stone Church was ten years old. But the passion to plant a church had come much earlier in my life, when I was just sixteen. At that time I was trying to find stability because I was the product of a pretty messed-up family. As I mentioned earlier, my parents divorced in the early 1970s, before it was very common. Though my parents had attended church since my early childhood, there were things that they never surrendered to God, and that destroyed their marriage and our family. After the divorce, my life descended into misery. The three most significant men in my life left me: my dad and my two older brothers, who eventually went to live with him. I lived with my mom and my younger sister, and we felt completely on our own. We lived in government-subsidized housing. Dad sent little money, and Mom was a high school dropout who worked minimum-wage jobs to help us survive.

We struggled financially, but not in faith, which Mom modeled in both word and action. She used to tell me that God had more for me, if I was willing to listen to Him and fully follow Him. Meanwhile, she pursued God diligently, served in the church, and honored God with the first 10 percent, the tithe, of everything she earned, despite our poverty. Though I had come to Christ at age nine, the struggles of our family marked me, and I dreamed about a better life materially. I hoped to be an attorney someday. I wanted to be somebody and do something important. But I also sensed that God wanted me to become a pastor.

The most marking moment of my life and faith occurred in the fall of 1977. I was sitting alone in my room, talking to God and trying to figure out what direction to take in my life. I had little experience learning how to distinguish God's prompts from my own wishes, but I wanted to make a decision—once and for all—concerning what I would do in my career. So, with all the wisdom of my sixteen years, I told God, "I'm going to pick up my Bible, open it at random, and put my finger on a verse. If you want me to be a pastor, then you have to make it clear to me. Otherwise, I'm going to become an attorney." By the way, I don't recommend that. But God, in His mercy, often takes care of the young and the foolish. At that time, I was both.

I closed my eyes, opened my Bible, and put my finger on a page. When I looked down, this is what my finger was pointing to:

And you will be called priests of the LORD,
you will be named ministers of our God.

I was stunned. It was Isaiah 61:6. I quickly went to the beginning of the chapter and read,

The Spirit of the Sovereign LORD *is on me,*
because the LORD *has anointed me*
to preach good news to the poor.
He has sent me to bind up the brokenhearted,
to proclaim freedom for the captives
and release from darkness for the prisoners,
to proclaim the year of the LORD'*s favor . . .*
They will be called oaks of righteousness,
a planting of the LORD
for the display of his splendor.[5]

That was it; I was done. God couldn't have made my calling any clearer. My dream and His dream for me were now one and the same. I put away any thought of becoming a lawyer, and I did the only thing I knew to do in that moment as a teenager. I wrote the date and time in the Bible as my "YES" to God: November 13, 1977, at 10:55 p.m.

During that season of my life, I later had what could be called two "visions" from God. The first is hard to explain because God used the image of a fun house. Our family had often visited a theme park called Cedar Point when I was growing up. Among the various attractions was a simple fun house filled with things like slanted floors, a room of mirrors, and an upside-down room. To exit the fun house, you'd crawl onto a dark slide that spiraled down and dumped you into the sand outside. I never really cared for that slide; though it was fun, it was also dark and claustrophobic.

Exaltation of the Afflicted.

CHAPTER 61

Nov. 13, 1977
10:55 p.m.

THE ^aSpirit of the Lord ¹GOD is upon me,
  Because the LORD has anointed me
  To bring good news to the ^{2b}afflicted;
  He has sent me to ^cbind up the brokenhearted,
  To ^dproclaim liberty to captives,
  And ³freedom to prisoners;

2 To ^aproclaim the favorable year of the LORD,
  And the ^bday of vengeance of our God;
  To ^ccomfort all who mourn,

3 To ^agrant those who mourn in Zion,
  Giving them a garland instead of ashes,
  The ^boil of gladness instead of mourning,
  The mantle of praise instead of a spirit of fainting.
  So they will be called ^{1c}oaks of righteousness,
  The planting of the LORD, that He may be glorified.

4 Then they will ^arebuild the ancient ruins,
  They will raise up the former devastations,
  And they will repair the ruined cities,
  The desolations of many generations.

5 And ^astrangers will stand and pasture your flocks,
  And ¹foreigners will be your farmers and your vinedressers.

6 But you will be called the ^apriests of the LORD;
  You will be spoken of as ^bministers of our God.
  You will eat the ^cwealth of nations,
  And in their ¹riches you will boast.

7 Instead of your shame *you will have a* double *portion,*
  And *instead of* humiliation they will shout for joy over
    their portion.
  Therefore they will possess a double *portion* in their
    land,
  ^aEverlasting joy will be theirs.

8 For I, the LORD, ^alove justice,
  I hate robbery ¹in the burnt offering;
  And I will faithfully give them their recompense,
  And I will make an ^beverlasting covenant with them.

9 Then their offspring will be known among the nations,
  And their descendants in the midst of the peoples.
  All who see them will recognize them
  Because they are the offspring *whom* the LORD has
    blessed.

10 I will ^arejoice greatly in the LORD,
  My soul will exult in ^bmy God;
  For He has ^cclothed me with garments of salvation,
  He has wrapped me with a robe of righteousness,
  As a bridegroom decks himself with a garland,
  And as a bride adorns herself with her jewels.

11 For as the earth brings forth its sprouts,
  And as a garden causes the things sown in it to spring up,
  So the Lord ¹GOD will ^acause ^brighteousness and praise
  To spring up before all the nations.

1 ¹YHWH, usually
rendered LORD ²Or,
humble ³Lit., *opening to
those who are bound-*
^aIs. 11:2; 48:16; Luke 4:18,
19 ^bIs. 11:4; 28:19; 32:7 ^cIs.
57:15 ^dIs. 42:7; 49:9

2 ^aIs. 49:8; 60:10 ^bIs.
2:12; 13:6; 34:2, 8 ^cIs.
57:18; Jer. 31:13; Matt. 5:4

3 ¹Or, *terebinths*
^aIs. 60:20 ^bPs. 23:5; 45:7
104:15 ^cIs. 60:21; Jer.
17:7, 8

4 ^aIs. 49:8; 58:12; Ezek.
36:33; Amos 9:14

5 ¹Lit., *sons of the
foreigner*
^aIs. 14:2; 60:10

6 ¹Or, *glory*
^aIs. 66:21 ^bIs. 56:6 ^cIs. 60:5,
11

7 ^aPs. 16:11

8 ¹Or, *with iniquity*
^aIs. 5:16; 28:17; 30:18 ^bIs.
55:3; Gen. 17:7; Ps. 105:10;
Jer. 32:40

10 ^aIs. 12:1, 2; 25:9; 4:16;
51:3 ^bIs. 49:4 ^cIs. 49:18;
52:1

11 ¹YHWH, usually
rendered LORD
^aIs. 45:23, 24; 60:18, 21 ^bPs.
72:3; 85:11

1041

I explain all that because in this vision I was at the top of this slide and an endless line of people were coming through the fun house and passing me to get on the slide. But I understood that this meant something spiritual. It was symbolic. The slide led down to a horrible eternity without God. People were dismissing God and indulging self in an effort to fulfill their life dreams, yet they had bought into a lie. I was painfully aware that they were laughing their way to their doom.

In the vision, God had placed me at the slide entrance to rescue people from the slide. And the burden of their misled version of fun and impending doom was so heavy on me that I was weeping. I was begging and pleading to keep people from getting onto that slide.

When I awoke from the vision, God simply said, "This is your life purpose. People will chase things in this world like it's a fun house and get on the slide to an eternity without me. I want you to carry the burden of one who knows what's at stake. Reach as many people as possible and deter them from going down the slide."

I drew a picture of that vision, and it's been sealed in my mind ever since. I knew that it was my job to communicate God's love and offer of eternal life, and that I was to someday plant a church with that purpose.

The second vision was of a very large auditorium, a coliseum-style space filled with thousands of people. When someone came up to speak, it totally shocked me, because it wasn't the person I expected. It was me! And for some reason, I knew that there was a number attached to that picture: eleven thousand. I have to admit that I've never fully understood that number. At the time, I guessed that God was telling me the church I led would be huge someday. (The largest church I'd seen at that time was two or three hundred people.) I'm still not sure what everything in the vision meant, but here's what I concluded at the time: *God, you have given me a dream to plant a church that will reach thousands of spiritually unresolved people. You want me to help thousands discover your dream for their life. I'm all in. I will give my life in pursuit of that vision, and I'll serve you because I believe you will do this.*

Trust me, I know these are unusual experiences. Most people don't receive an actual vision from God, much less two of them. And most people aren't naive enough to base the most important decision of their life on a game of Bible roulette. But everyone is called by God. Everyone is invited by God to come to Him through Jesus Christ. And everyone who accepts God's invitation is drawn to Him and is called to a purpose.

John's Perspective

I believe God desires for us to be successful. But I believe God's definition of *success* is different from the world's. To be successful, we don't need to be rich. We don't need to be famous. We don't even need to be happy. Success is...

Knowing God and His purpose for our lives,
Growing to reach our maximum potential, and
Sowing seeds that benefit others.

That's the kind of success anyone can achieve, God being their helper.

God has dreams for everyone's life. And believe it or not, if you're willing to follow God and be true to yourself, you'll discover that the dreams you have for your life and God's dream for you can be one and the same.

Dreams Sometimes Play Out Differently than We Expect

If you get a call and vision from God at sixteen years old and you pursue God with all your heart—even if you come from a dysfunctional messed-up family—then God will do His part and make it happen, right? You'll live happily ever after!

Not exactly.

Jump forward ten years to 1987. I had completed Bible college, earned my degree, and married Marcia, my college sweetheart and the love of my life. I was twenty-six years old and working as a pastor. By then I had been in ministry for a decade, first as a volunteer leader and then successfully as a staff pastor at Kentwood Community Church (outside my hometown of Grand Rapids, Michigan). I had paid my dues, I had gained experience, I had done well at Kentwood, and the time had finally come to fulfill God's vision by planting the church God had shown me as a teenager.

Marcia and I left our home in Kentwood, Michigan, and relocated to Gwinnett County, Georgia, northeast of Atlanta, the place we believed God had pointed us to. In preparation for planting the church, we had done everything experts said to do. We had saved money. We had the blessing and support of our church in Kentwood to help us get started. We had recruited three families to join us in the move to Georgia. We were ready.

As soon as we moved into our apartment down south, we got to work. With the help of our team, we visited four to five thousand homes and made twenty thousand phone calls to people in the community. We asked questions about people's spiritual interests and invited anyone without a home church to attend our first service. We gathered together a core group of twenty local people and started meeting with them in our apartment. We even had people receive Christ in our living room before the church officially opened. After all those preparations, we were finally ready to launch the church.

More than eight hundred people in the community had said they would attend the service on opening Sunday. I rented a movie theater with 440 seats, figuring about half of the people who said they planned to come would attend. That would be a great start for a church.

The morning of the first service finally arrived. And when I stepped out onstage, I was greeted by a crowd of... sixty-nine people. Add the kids and workers and we had 104 people total. That was not the life-changing opening day I had pictured. I had hoped to make an impact on the community. But the impact that was made that day was on me. I couldn't see the people who had come. All I could see were the 371 empty seats! Fear gripped me that day in a way I had never known. Not the kind of fear that goes away after a rough game. I'm talking about a fear that threatens to crush the hopes, dreams, and desires of your heart. It was the kind of fear that displaces faith in the core of your soul—the fear that eats away at your confidence bit by bit.

Maybe you've known that kind of fear. Perhaps you're living with it right now. And perhaps that makes you quick to dismiss any hope of having a home run life. You know what the "empty seats" are in your life. Maybe your family growing up was as imperfect as mine—or even worse. Or you dreamed of a full marriage but it feels empty. Or you dreamed of a full career adventure, but it came up empty. Or you opened a new business but made half of what you needed to survive. Or you were actually successful and you hoped it would be fulfilling, yet it has left you feeling empty inside.

My expectations for our grand opening had been huge; my results had not. Then the next week, half as many people showed up!

We ended up being a small church of about fifty people. All I could see ahead of me was struggle. I didn't want to fight the small but difficult battles of breaking the hundred-people barrier, then the two-hundred-people barrier. I wanted to start with critical mass. And I expected to. After all, God had given me a vision for thousands. You can't start that small and ever hope to reach large! What was happening to the dream?

Fear tightened its grip. I thought, *What if the church never grows? What if we never reach people for God? What if my deepest fears are true—that my life won't matter? What if I get stuck in a marginal job,*

in a small church, on the sidelines of life, doing nothing of real impor-
tance and never making a significant impact? What if my life is a fail-
ure, the dream a mirage? The very thought of it paralyzed me.

I wish I could tell you that I snapped out of it. But I can't. For the next several years, the church struggled. And so did I. I hit nothing but walls in my leadership. And it took every penny we had to keep the church afloat. Marcia and I, who by then were the parents of two small children, emptied our savings account to survive. We lost our house; we lost our two newer cars and settled for one very used one. After three years of this, the church was broke and so were we.

Then it got worse. We lost our health insurance. I can't explain the intensity and depth of my discouragement. "Okay, God," I prayed, "you took us from Michigan to Georgia and didn't bother to come with us. You've let all our dreams crash and burn. I'm practically bankrupt, and you can't seem to change that," I ranted. "Can you at least keep my family healthy until we can get health insurance in six months?"

The answer was no. Almost immediately our daughter got seri-ously ill and we racked up thousands of dollars in hospital bills. I had to sign a promissory note to get her treated. *Great,* I thought, *now I can add financial failure to my career failure.*

I suppose the bottom of my descent into broken dreams came when I asked Marcia to go back to work. I had promised her that once we had kids, she could leave the workplace and pour herself into the kids full-time. But we were desperate. I felt humiliated. I couldn't even pro-vide for my family! Marcia went back to work.

I had already been doing side jobs to help keep us afloat, but now I had to do more. I went to the public library and found a DIY videotape teaching how to install tile. I studied it. Then I quietly took construc-tion jobs at night tiling restaurant kitchens to bring in income without telling anyone.

More time passed, and still we struggled.

In 1991, after nearly four years of living like this, I was done.

Meeting in various rented facilities, we had grown from fifty people to eighty-two. I was ready to close down the church and abandon my dream. I was defeated. I was a failure. My leadership was ineffective. We were on the brink of personal bankruptcy. I was taking the stress out on my wife. And I just couldn't keep lying to myself, saying, *Any minute the church is going to turn around*. I was striking out, and the evidence was overwhelming: God wasn't going to give me a home run. The dream was dead.

Broken and humiliated, I drove back to Grand Rapids to talk to Wayne Schmidt, my old boss at Kentwood Community Church where I had been successful on staff. I sat in his office and spilled my guts. I told him about the pain of our situation. I told him I had failed. And I gathered what little courage I had left to ask him one question: Would he be willing to give me back my old job?

"Yes," he said, "but not right now." For a fleeting second I had hope; then I started to feel numb. "I think you are exactly where God wants you," he said kindly. He encouraged me to give it more time to stabilize. I wanted to say, *I just don't have it in me*, but I sat there silently. Then he closed with something I will never forget: "Kevin," he said, "if you've lost your faith, then borrow mine."

I returned home confused and defeated. What was I going to do? I couldn't go back, I couldn't go on, yet I couldn't quit, either. What in the world was I to do?

What Should We Do with Our Broken Dreams?

That's where many of us find ourselves at some point in life. We don't want to give up, yet we don't know how to move forward. When we're kids, people tell us, "You can become anything you want!" It sounds good—until we grow up. Then we discover that many of our dreams will go unfulfilled. That's true of Christians as well as non-believers.

We tell people that Jesus is the answer—and He is—but even if we've embraced Him, we can still find ourselves in such a discouraging place.

Maybe that's where you are. Did you expect a full life, but instead all you see is a bunch of "empty seats"? Are your dreams coming true, or are you convinced that dreams are appropriate only for children and the deluded? Is there hope, or do you believe you need to settle for what you have and pretend you're content?

Many Christians do exactly that. But I don't think that's where God wants us. Life without any kind of dream is a loss. Then again, life with a dream that you can never achieve feels like a living hell. We don't have the power to *make* our dreams come true, so where does that leave us?

In such circumstances, some people "try" God for a while but quit when they don't get instant happiness. Others try a second marriage, but a second marriage is usually even harder than a first. Other people spend money. Or they abuse substances in their search for relief from their disappointment and pain. They end up in debt or addicted. Some people do all of the above.

If you're a person of faith and you've found yourself in a place where your dreams have been unfulfilled, what does it mean? Does it mean that Christianity simply *does not work*? Does it mean you should *give up*? Does it mean you simply need to *try harder*? And if you're not a person of faith, does it mean it's all on you to create a home run life?

The answers to these questions, the rest of the Maxwell mentoring story, and the discovery of God's design for a home run life lie in the chapters that follow. What seemed hopeless for so long turned to hope. What I did not know at the time was that God was revealing how He grows us up for His bigger picture. What I didn't know until later was that there is a definable, specific pattern that God uses to grow our lives, help us reach our dreams, and raise us up as leaders. To use the baseball metaphor, it's how God enables us to have a home run life.

If no one has ever shown you the process God uses to grow us up and make us successful according to His values, then you're going to love the next couple of chapters. They will forever change the way you see and do life. Not sure you believe that? Well, if you've lost your faith, then borrow some of mine. God really does have more for you!

John's Application Guide

Discussion Questions

1. Kevin mentioned in the chapter that many Christians' lives seem to fall far short of their expectations and what God desires for them. Have you also observed that to be true? If so, why do you think these things happen?
2. God gave Kevin visions that have guided the direction of his life. What is your reaction to that? Can you relate to it? Explain. If not, how has God guided you? What have you drawn upon for direction in your life?
3. When you were a child, what did you dream of doing or becoming as an adult?
4. What are your dreams now?
5. Have you ever experienced an "empty seats" moment, when a dream seemed to be dead or dying? How did you respond?
6. What is your response to the statements about there being more in us and for us from God? Do you genuinely believe them to be true? What self-limiting beliefs do you currently hold, and what are you willing to do to overcome them?

Assignment

Plan to carve out a whole day, a half day, or at least a couple of hours from your normal routine to have an extended prayer time with God. Set a date and time on your calendar. If you do not own a journal, notebook, Moleskine, or similar item for writing down your prayers and capturing your observations, then buy one

(Continued)

beforehand. Take it, a pen or pencil, a Bible, and anything else you might need (such as water) to a quiet place that you know will be conducive to having a conversation with God. While there, use your journal to write out your prayers. Be sure to...

1. Acknowledge to God that He is God and you are not.
2. Talk to God about the things that are currently on your mind.
3. Talk to God about past, current, and future dreams.
4. Ask Him to reveal to you whether you are on His agenda or your own.
5. Ask Him to give you direction for your life and to reveal His will.
6. Ask Him to reveal His dream for your life.

When you do these things, don't expect to receive answers to all your questions. It's been our experience that God usually reveals His will slowly over time as we take steps of obedience to His prompting. Depending on your history, this may represent first steps in the pursuit of God, or it may merely be the opening of a new chapter. Either way, follow through.

3

God's Game Plan for Winning at Life

*H*opeless. That's the best word to describe how I felt during the drive back home to Atlanta from Michigan in 1991 after failing to get my old job back at Kentwood Community Church. Wayne had encouraged me to have hope, but he didn't give me a job. Nothing seemed to be any better than before I visited him.

Could I actually borrow someone else's faith? The idea intrigued me. If so, how?

After I got home, I pulled together the fifteen core leaders of the church and confessed that I was ready to close the doors.

"I can't keep doing this," I explained. "God has to change the church and make it grow, or He has to change me!" We had eighty-two people after four years of work. And I had thought our launch day was a failure! "I'm obviously striking out and I can't see what God is doing," I told them. "So let's pray for the next two or three months. If God doesn't change something or change me, I'm closing the church!"

I had already been desperately seeking God by going to a retreat center every Tuesday at 6 a.m. to pray, journal, and read Scripture. My mom, always wanting to help me, paid the fees for this, and I had been doing it for *three years*! I was hoping for answers, but God had been silent. Now I was inviting others to pray with me.

During one of my prayer times in 1991, I was expressing my frustration and found myself saying, "God, you owe me! I have spent my life since age nine following you. I left the security of home to plant a church in Atlanta, and you are letting my life sink into the pit. I've given up everything for you! How could you let this become my life? You owe me!"

"Kevin," I sensed God saying, "I do not owe you. I *own* you." That was a startling moment. God was patiently reshaping my perspective. I felt like I was being shaken from a nightmare and waking up. It was sobering and clarifying at the same time. An eerie awareness settled on my soul. Perhaps I had spent my life saying, "It's all about God," when what I had been living actually said, "It's all about me."

What came to my mind in that moment was Hebrews 11, the chapter that lists the giants of the faith. They fell into two groups: The first were mentioned by name. They passed through the Red Sea on dry land, conquered kingdoms, shut the mouths of lions, became powerful in battle, and received back their dead raised to life. The second group consisted of the faithful who were not named. They were tortured, flogged, imprisoned, stoned, and sawn in two. Many wandered in deserts or hid in caves or lived in holes in the ground.

I have always heard preachers talk about the first group and I had imagined that I would be named among them. And for the first time it was dawning on me, *What if I'm in the second group?* They were just as faith-filled. God was just as pleased with them as He was the ones named in Hebrews 11. If God *owns me*, He can put me in either group.

Now what was I going to do? Would I serve God or would I expect God to serve me? Did He owe me or own me? I finally broke. "Okay, God," I prayed. "I'm in. I'll do whatever you ask, even if it means leading eighty-two people for the rest of my life!" And then I told God something that I shared with no one else—not even my wife. "Since age sixteen I've held on to the dream you gave me of reaching thousands. But I quit. I can't believe it anymore. And I'm laying it down.

I will no longer believe that it was a vision from you unless you do something as radical as give me a leadership mentor. And I mean a real one, someone like John Maxwell. And for that matter, I'm never going to ask. You'll have to ask this person for me, and he'll have to offer. So the day that a John Maxwell says, 'Hey Kevin, I believe God has asked me to mentor you,' then on that day I'll believe and pick up the vision again."

And that was the end of it. I never spoke of it again. I had nearly forgotten until the moment of the bus trip. It's curious how God works. I follow a simple prompt to attend a leadership conference, John comes to a simple dinner, we have a simple prayer after dinner, and God does a supernatural thing. It was a home run moment in life!

So now you know why I could not regain my emotional or spiritual composure on the ride home. God had delivered the more He had for me. As at no other time in my life, I discovered the truth of *never put a period where God puts a comma.*

It's entirely possible that you are reading this book at a time when you have placed a period on a dream, but God has not. Many of us have experienced the disappointment, loss, grief, anger, blame, and brokenness of a failed business, a job loss, infertility, a failed marriage, family fallout, health threats, prodigal children, financial hardship, character crashes, and broken dreams. So what is God doing when we are following Him but striking out without hope? Is it just game over?

John's Perspective

Jeremiah 29:11 says, "'For I know the plans I have for you,' declares the LORD, 'plans to prosper you and not to harm you, plans to give you hope and a future.'" God is always faithful, even if we are not. If you have God, there is always hope.

(Continued)

Even the word *hope* should be an encouragement to us. The Hebrew word *hope* comes from the root word for *rope*. The image is of a rope stretching toward the future. As long as we hold on to that rope and are guided by it toward God's future for us, our hope should be strong.

Maybe we put a period on our dreams or on our life purpose when God doesn't intend us to. What if all along, God was still at work while things weren't going as you'd hoped and planned? What if God was using *strikeout* seasons to train us for home run hitting? What if God was using powerlessness to grow us up?

The Power of Powerlessness

As human beings, we don't like powerlessness. We want to have our way. We want to be in control. We want to choose our path and purpose, and then fulfill it. But our desire to control our own destiny can have a way of making us act like mini gods. And the problem? We aren't God. And it's frustrating to try to be God without the power of God.

That doesn't mean we should do nothing. We have decisions to make as we move through life, and they have a major impact on our lives. But the free will given to mankind does not undo the sovereignty of God. Somehow, while exercising His will and letting us make our own choices, He still manages to fulfill His purpose. I don't know about you, but that concept is too big for my brain to wrap around. I have met people and read books claiming to have God all figured out, but I'm not convinced.

What I am sure of is that God wants only the best for us. And like a loving parent, He is restoring us to His image. In that journey, He has never promised to tell us everything He's up to while He's running the universe. That's part of our problem—because we always want to know. If we have any kind of leadership bent, that desire to know is compelling.

This desire to understand God and His workings is as old as humankind. It was present in the Garden of Eden. And it's evident in the book of Job, one of the oldest writings in the Bible. Job believed he was living a righteous life, yet he suffered horrible calamity: the death of his children, the loss of his possessions, and untold pain and physical suffering. His wife told him to curse God and die. His friends admonished him to confess his hidden sin. Job revered God, but he wanted to know what God was up to. Job felt he couldn't go on, yet he wouldn't quit on God. Only when Job recognized his own powerlessness was he able to accept his life. And in the end, God had new dreams for Job. And what we might call a home run life.

Remember David? He had a similar experience, recognizing his own powerlessness. He saw evil men who dismissed God living in prosperity. Meanwhile he tried to follow God wholeheartedly, and he often suffered. It didn't seem right—especially from the point of view of someone called and anointed by God to lead! Yet he learned that the only power he had was to throw himself at God's feet and depend on Him.

All those years while I was trying to build the church, God had been waiting for me to recognize my powerlessness and...give up—give up my agenda for His, give up trying to *be* someone through success, give up pursuing my own glory, give up my willfulness so that I could do His will. Why? So He could build me! Giving up was the breakthrough God had been waiting for, and finally He was free to help me to change, to learn, and to grow.

I didn't want to lead a small church, but a small church isn't insignificant to God. Every person in my small church mattered to Him. They are His children. God doesn't withhold His love from any people because of where they are or what they can or can't do. He loves people the way I love my own children—because they are mine and I delight in them. God feels that way about them, and about you, and about me.

My breakdown had finally led to a breakthrough. For the first time in a long time, I was reminded of God's character. God is ...

Too mysterious for me to define,
Too obvious for me to deny,
Too great for me to manage,
Too loving for me to mistrust,
Too mighty for me to dismiss,
Too powerful for me to battle,
Too fatherly for me to forget,
Too kind for me to ignore, and
Too right for me to go wrong.

The only thing I could do was trust Him and learn to depend on Him. I was *finally* putting myself in a place where God could grow me up.

Most of the climbs we try to make in life—faith, marriage, parenting, career, leadership—eventually take us to the end of ourselves, where we finally realize we are powerless. When we reach that point of exhaustion (and for some people, it takes a *really* long time), we are ready for God to do something in our lives. We finally admit we do not have peace in our souls and we have to let God lead. We can only change, grow, and have life to the full if we are willing to become dependent on God and turn to Him. This is true for every follower of Christ, and for every spiritually mature leader. It is the *only* way we can fulfill our calling and purpose.

Once I stopped pursuing my own glory, something became clear to me: God was not killing the dream in me; He was killing my ego! He was not taking me out of the game; He was training me *for* the game.

He was not chopping down the tree of my life and career; He was growing my roots. I realized that maybe—just maybe—God is more interested in how deep we grow our roots than how big we grow our branches. After all, the quality of a tree's fruit is more dependent on the health of its roots than the height of its limbs. God was building me into a person He could use.

How God Grows Us Up

I was finally open to anything God had for me, but then the question I was asking myself was, *Now what? Where is God leading, and how do I move forward?* I felt like someone trying to put together a puzzle without the picture. If you've ever tried to put a puzzle together, you know the importance of the picture on the box top. Being handed two hundred pieces of a puzzle and trying to put them together without knowing the big picture seems nearly impossible. My life and the pursuit of God had become a collection of pieces for a puzzle I could not put together. Maybe you've felt that way, too.

Two things helped me during this time. The first was the mentoring time I had with John Maxwell. He would give me a few meetings a year to ask him leadership questions. There were no restrictions and no question was out of bounds, just wide-open conversation. It was— and still is—an awesome experience.

The second was perhaps the kindest thing God the Father did for me in this season. He gave me the big picture of how God grows up His people and His leaders. I discovered that there was in fact a knowable, specific, consistent pattern that I could follow to remake me into God's image. The seed of this is in Romans 12:1–2. The passage says, "I urge you, brothers and sisters, in view of God's mercy, to offer your bodies as a living sacrifice, holy and pleasing to God—this is your true and proper worship. Do not conform to the pattern of this world, but be transformed by the renewing of your mind. Then you will be able to test and approve what God's will is—his good, pleasing and perfect will."

So what is God's pattern? I found it in the story of Joseph. If you've read the book of Genesis, then you undoubtedly remember what happened in Joseph's life. He was one of twelve brothers raised in a God-fearing family, the great-grandson of Abraham, with whom God had made His covenant. Joseph grew up hearing the stories of God's interaction with Abraham, Isaac, and Jacob, his father. If we were to draw a parallel between Joseph's story and today's culture, we might say that Joseph was a guy who grew up in church.

Joseph was favored by God. He was also his dad's favorite. That didn't go over well with his brothers. In fact, in time, they grew to hate him. And Joseph made things worse when at age seventeen he shared God's dream for his life. Genesis says,

> Joseph had a dream, and when he told it to his brothers, they hated him all the more. He said to them, "Listen to this dream I had: We were binding sheaves of grain out in the field when suddenly my sheaf rose and stood upright, while your sheaves gathered around mine and bowed down to it."
>
> His brothers said to him, "Do you intend to reign over us? Will you actually rule us?" And they hated him all the more because of his dream and what he had said.
>
> Then he had another dream, and he told it to his brothers. "Listen," he said, "I had another dream, and this time the sun and moon and eleven stars were bowing down to me."[1]

It seemed certain to Joseph that he was going to do great things. He was going to be important. And he had every reason to believe that God would bring his dreams to fruition.

We might expect Joseph to immediately become the leader of

his family and rule them with wisdom and grace. But God often takes His people in a direction different from the expected. God is true to His promises, but not to our timetable or game plan. He wants us to dream—and dream big—but He doesn't want us to try to wrest control from Him for how it plays out. In the case of Joseph, instead of ruling his brothers, he was tossed into a pit by them and then sold into slavery. Talk about things not turning out the way you expected!

When Joseph saw himself standing and the others bowing, he probably said to himself, *This makes sense. I am the great-grandson of the great Abraham, whom God promised to make into a great nation. My father is rich. And of all his children, I am the favorite. He gave me the special coat to set me apart. It's likely I'm going to be a great man.* Joseph thought he was going to be a ruler, and God would simply make it happen. The problem was that Joseph thought it was all about him. (That, I must admit, was also me! How about you?) Instead, Joseph became a slave, a piece of property—in Egypt, of all places. He was in an alien environment, far from home, having to learn a new language and adapt to a new culture.

I wonder how long it took him to realize that nobody was going to come looking for him—not his father, whom his brothers convinced Joseph was dead. Not his brothers, who hated him enough to want to kill him. No one! The question was: What would he do? He couldn't go back; he couldn't go forward; and he didn't want to give up. Joseph was in a place perhaps all of us can relate to.

The Four Growth Gates

When you know someone's story ends in the equivalent of a grand-slam home run, you may be tempted to skip over all the strikeouts they experience. In baseball, Babe Ruth was known as the home run king—with 714. Relatively few people knew that when he retired, he was also the strikeout king—with 1,330 strikeouts, the record in 1935.

When Joseph was sold into slavery, he was starting to feel what it was like to strike out, yet God had not abandoned him. Everything looked wrong to Joseph, but everything was right with God. Joseph had begun to travel a journey that neither he nor anyone else would ever have suspected was being guided by the hand of God. His redemption, learning, and ultimate success came because he passed through four growth gates that demonstrate how God wants us to live. I believe it is God's pattern for living—His game plan, as it were—as opposed to the pattern of this world.

Win Dependence

The first growth gate people must go though to follow God's pattern is dependence on God. (It is also the last growth gate, but I'm getting ahead of myself. I'll discuss that in chapter 9.) Joseph started to learn dependence the moment he was dropped into the pit, and the lessons continued for him as a purchased slave in the house of Potiphar.

When Joseph landed in the pit, I bet he prayed. Wouldn't you? Haven't you prayed from the pits? Haven't you begged God to rescue you from a hole in life? He was only seventeen years old. Oh, how he must have wept! How he must have pleaded with his brothers. How he must have experienced shock, disbelief, confusion, anger, grief, and sorrow upon sorrow into utter hopelessness. What may have been the last words of his brothers must have echoed through his head: "We'll see what comes of his dreams."

God did not immediately rescue Joseph. Instead, God let Joseph lose for a season. Joseph was stripped of everything he would've depended upon to accomplish the dream.

He was stripped of his coat, which made him look and feel important. He was stripped of his name and the security of his father's resources and heritage. He was stripped of everything familiar—from family and friends to language and worship, all that provided community and stability. He was stripped of his freedom, his human dignity, his options. And he was stripped of his influence and affluence—all within minutes.

When we get into one of life's pits and God does not rescue us the way we expect, we wonder what God's doing. We think He's left us. But God was with Joseph. What if God was simply teaching Joseph how to win dependence? He needed to learn now to depend upon God for the dream. This is the first and most important growth gate for life to the full, a life filled with home runs. It's also the most difficult. Why? Because the supernatural is just the opposite of the natural.

Let me illustrate. In the natural world, growing up means becoming more independent. We are born completely dependent upon our parents. We cannot feed ourselves, clothe or dress ourselves, comfort ourselves, or provide for ourselves. After a while we begin learning to put food in our mouths, speak, get dressed, and make little decisions. Our parents still provide for us, but over time we're expected to become more and more independent. Eventually, we must become independent, self-reliant, and free from our parents.

I tend to agree with those who say God makes our kids young and cute so we want to provide for them and can't imagine their leaving. Then He makes them teenagers so we want them to provide for themselves and we can't imagine their staying. I keep telling my nine-year-old Jadon to stay nine and live with me forever. But I used to say that to Jake, who's now eighteen. I don't want the eighteen-year-old to stay around forever. I want him to become like his older brother Josh, who is twenty-four, a college graduate, married, and on his own.

In the spiritual world, growing up means doing the opposite: We need to learn to become more *dependent*. We are born in sin and possess a spirit of independence from God. We tend to disregard Him as Creator (as if we came out of nothing), set our own moral standards, and make decisions with our own wisdom. We start out far from God, but when we are spiritually reborn we become dependent upon God our Father in heaven.[2]

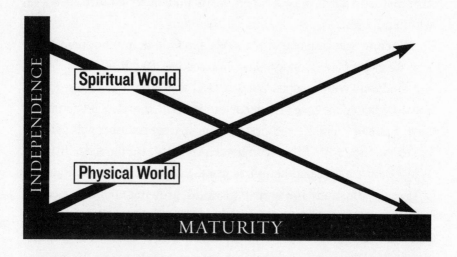

Spiritual growth is the process of moving from independence to dependence. That's what Jesus was teaching when He said, "I am the vine; you are the branches. If you remain in me and I in you, you will bear much fruit; apart from me you can do nothing."[3] This is a deep truth that takes most people a lifetime of lessons to mature into. If you don't understand that this is how you grow up spiritually, then you'll still think God exists to help you with your agenda. But God does not join *us* to help with our agenda; we join *Him*. He's the source of life to the full. We may be able to pull off a success or two with our talent, but there is no real peace for the soul or winning in the whole of life or in the hereafter without the author of life. Growing up supernaturally means becoming more and more dependent upon God.

King David of ancient Israel understood this. In Psalm 20 he wrote, "Some trust in chariots and some in horses, but we trust in the name of the Lord our God." He was declaring his dependence on God because he knew the spiritual world has more weight than the material world and God can move the chess pieces of life at will. God alone gives success, even in the battles of life.

Perhaps you've been puzzled by this growth gate. Perhaps like most people, when good things are happening, you say, "God is blessing me." But when you face difficulties, you wonder, "Where is God?" The parable of the sower in the Gospels describes people who fall away because of trials and others who become distracted by worries. Both types fail to grow into productive believers and leaders. But James said trials would help us to be "mature and complete."[4] If we are to become complete believers, complete followers, complete leaders, we must embrace trials, because God uses them to teach us how to depend on Him. When troubles come, we need to learn to lean into them, not avoid them, because by leaning in, we begin to depend on God. When we do that, God gets the credit.

I'm convinced that early on, though I was bent on getting tangible results, God was bent on teaching me to depend on Him. After I prayed for a couple of months in 1991 with the fifteen core church leaders, God asked two things of me: First, He wanted me to change how I thought. He asked me to quit measuring myself by the size of the church. Second, He wanted me to change how I prayed. God said, "Pray every Saturday night in renewed dependence and I will show up on Sunday."

Those were the only two things we did differently. And 12Stone doubled in the next two years. It may not seem like much, but when it takes more than four years to reach eighty-two people, then two years to reach 160 each weekend felt like hope. Learning to depend upon God will redefine your life and leadership.

Win Within

Joseph's journey reveals the next growth gate. People who follow God's game plan also win within. Let's be blunt: The quality of our relationships and the life we live will never consistently rise above the quality of character within us. We must win character battles if we hope to win at life, see our dreams fulfilled, and have peace deep in our soul.

God's dream for Joseph involved more than the worldly success of ruling over others. God's heart was to develop Joseph to be a person who could rule over himself. The greatest battles we face are not around us, but within us. And God so deeply loved Joseph that He was forming him from the inside out.

Recalling the details of Joseph's story, we remember that he ended up in the home of Potiphar, a military leader. Potiphar was a man of great power and influence. Despite being a mere slave, Joseph was able to thrive in this new environment. Scripture says, "The LORD was with Joseph so that he prospered, and he lived in the house of his Egyptian master. When his master saw that the LORD was with him and that the LORD gave him success in everything he did, Joseph found favor in his eyes and became his attendant."[5]

Despite the circumstances, things were looking up for Joseph. But then he faced a new trial: The boss's wife propositioned him. At that time, Joseph was a young man in his late teens or early twenties, which by definition means he had raging hormones. He was also far from home with no accountability. Let's not kid ourselves about how strong this temptation must have been for him! We can imagine Joseph thinking, *Well, why not? My brothers betrayed me. My father assumes I'm dead. I'm on my own. Nobody really knows me. I have no chance of getting married, and my dreams are dead. I might as well satisfy myself. After all, I have natural desires given by God, so why not? God wants me to be happy.*

Joseph had a decision to make. Would he depend on God and honor his values, or would he seize the moment to indulge his desires? Make no mistake: Joseph must have faced an incredible internal battle. This was his first real test of self-trust and self-leadership. And it's important to recognize that self-leadership always precedes the effective leadership of others. The war we all have to repeatedly win is within.

Joseph fled Potiphar's wife, leaving his coat behind. In that moment of temptation, he demonstrated that the faith of his forefathers and his father Jacob had become his own personal faith. In the forge of dependence, God had begun to hammer out Joseph's character. And when pressure came, he was able to withstand it and pass the test. He recognized in that moment that sleeping with Potiphar's wife would be more than just a betrayal of his boss, more than a mere lapse in judgment. It would be a sin against the God whom he had come to rely upon. Joseph was no longer chasing his dreams. He was chasing the God of his dreams—and depending on Him.

In 12Stone's first few years, I was unaware that God was more concerned about my being than my doing. I was trying to impress others and God in those years, while God was trying to impress His image upon me. God's desire was to remake what had been distorted by sin so that I could have life to the full, a home run life. He was not tearing down the dream He had given me; He was growing up the leader.

That's often what God is doing when it seems your career is crashing, your marriage is ending, and your future is hopeless. God is offering you a chance to grow. I came to realize that God was growing me through purity, obscurity, and insecurity. I had to hold on to my heart of purity. I had to learn the ego-killing lessons of obscurity. And God had to help me address my issues of insecurity.

Joseph did the right thing, yet he got punished for it. When Potiphar's wife lied, accusing him of doing the very thing she had proposed and he had refused to do, Joseph went from being a slave in a rich and powerful man's home to being a prisoner. Joseph certainly didn't want to walk that journey. Nobody would. But God was doing something in Joseph that could be developed no other way.

And that can also be true for us. There are things God wants to see come about in us that can only be developed by our going through trials and struggles. That's not because God doesn't love us. It's because God does love us. As Solomon, wisest of all leaders, wrote,

> *My son, do not despise the LORD's discipline*
> *and do not resent his rebuke,*
> *because the LORD disciplines those he loves,*
> *as a father the son he delights in.*[6]

Though we don't always understand what's happening to us, we can be confident that God is forming Himself in us. While we may be praying for material success, God wants to press us for spiritual substance. Are you willing to embrace this process? I hope so, because we must win within before we can proceed to the next growth gate.

Win with Others

People who win in life according to God's game plan win with others. They learn how to develop positive relationships with people. Joseph didn't have a very good track record in this area when he was young. He certainly didn't treat his brothers well. How badly must Joseph have treated them for them to want to kill him or tell their father he was dead? If he treated his family badly, I can only imagine how he treated their servants and others outside the household.

All that changed when God allowed Joseph to move from favored son to fallen slave. Where he once had servants attend to him, he became a servant attending to others, first in a rich man's house, then in a prison. Perhaps there was a moment when Joseph was down on his hands and knees cleaning floors when important people walked by and didn't notice him. That had to transform his thinking!

Maybe he thought, *God, how could you let me be in this position? I was once important! I was once the person walking by. How could you abandon my life to obscurity?*

Maybe God the Father responded something like this: "Joseph, you thought you were important; you walked by other people as if they did not matter. You thought of my favor upon your life as permission to think less of others. You valued yourself above everyone else. But I never thought less of the servants in your household. I did not love your brothers less than you. Everyone has a purpose. Joseph, you need to learn the value of each person, whether master or servant, Hebrew or Egyptian, prisoner or Pharaoh. Transform how you value people."

I must confess to having made the Joseph mistake in how I valued people. Prior to planting 12Stone, I served on staff at Kentwood Community Church. At that time it was a young church meeting in a school. In five years, the church grew from reaching 125 people a weekend to more than a thousand. We went through a major relocation project and built on fifty acres.

That was the good news. The bad news? I thought I had something to do with that success. I thought God had set me apart to be somebody, and the size of our church meant God valued me more. As a result, in my early to mid-twenties I was looking down on pastors with small churches of fifty to a hundred people and thinking less of them. Then I planted 12Stone, and even after five years I was that small-church pastor! In His patience, God taught me that His favor was not permission to think less of others. And He didn't value me less when I led a small church than He does now.

I can tell you this: There's nothing more clarifying than being in the place of the person you once dismissed. Maybe that's why Moses was so changed after forty years in the desert. D. L. Moody once said, "Moses spent his first forty years thinking he was somebody. He spent his second forty years learning he was a nobody. He spent his third forty years discovering what God can do with a nobody."

Because God allowed Joseph to be in a position to discover the sorrows, struggles, pits, and prisons of other people, he developed compassion and patience. Being on the same level with everyone else helped him figure out how to treat people with dignity, how to become a servant, how to care about others, and how to break free from self-absorption. Those are necessary qualities in a leader God wants to use.

It took twenty-two years for Joseph to go full circle and face his brothers again. That interaction shows how much he had grown. At the time the brothers came to him during the famine, Joseph was the second most powerful man in the world's most powerful nation. Only Pharaoh was more powerful than Joseph. And what happened? His brothers—the ones who intended to kill him, who sold him into slavery, who cut him off from his loving father and everything he knew—showed up because they were hungry, and they bowed down to him. In that moment, the memory of his dream must have come rushing back to him.

What would you have done to them in that moment? All he had to do was say the word, and his servants would have put his brothers to death. Or made them slaves. Instead, Joseph valued them. He did the kind of thing that God the Father would do. He forgave them, releasing them from the consequences of their actions. By following God all those years and truly depending on Him, Joseph had become more like God: gracious and kind and loving and giving. Joseph summed up his perspective after Jacob's death, when his brothers came to him fearing revenge: "Don't be afraid. Am I in the place of God? You intended to harm me, but God intended it for good to accomplish what is now being done, the saving of many lives. So then, don't be afraid. I will provide for you and your children."[7]

That's how God wants us to treat others, and yet that is one of our greatest challenges: loving other people. It was no small lesson for Joseph, and it's no small lesson for most of us. We can try to gut our way through it, but if that's how we try to do it, we're destined to fail. Only by depending on God and developing godly character do we have the power to love others for a full life.

Win Results

Joseph learned dependence on God, he developed godly character, and he grew in his love for people in a way that honored God. But he wasn't done. To be complete in God's way of doing things for life to the full, there is still the fourth and final gate: getting results. People who follow God's game plan win results. To fulfill his purpose, Joseph had to be able to actually do something of value. He had to do the work God had created him to do. We see that come into play again and again in Joseph's story.

Scripture says, "The LORD was with him" and "gave him success in everything he did" when he was in Potiphar's house.[8] And again when he was in prison, it says, "The LORD was with Joseph and gave him success in whatever he did."[9] The favor of God was on Joseph, and he was highly competent. If you're going to be a slave, you might as well be the best!

Joseph wasn't competent when he was seventeen. It took time for him to become skilled and effective. God put Joseph in places where he could learn, grow, and develop. He learned the language and customs of Egypt in Potiphar's household. Then he learned how to administer the household and lead the other servants. He learned to run the prison for the warden. His increasing competence advanced him in Potiphar's house, in the prison, and with the cupbearer and baker. The world took notice because results matter, and Joseph was good.

It took thirteen years to prepare Joseph for the work he would eventually do—the fulfillment of the vision. Joseph was not just passing the time. He was engaged in preparation. Only after this training did Joseph get his shot—a chance to interpret a dream that none of the wise men in Egypt could decipher. By then, Joseph understood that it was only with God's help that he was able to accomplish anything of value. He had traveled the entire spiritual journey: He won dependence, won within, won with others, and won results. By preparing for the coming famine during the abundant years, he saved Egypt and the nation of Israel.

I'm often asked, "What would you have done differently in the early days of 12Stone to escape the long, slow, painful stages of growth?" After all, it took us into our seventh year to break the two-hundred-person barrier on a weekend. (And note that 80 percent of all church plants no longer exist by the fifth year.) So what would I do different? Nothing! Like Joseph, I believe God had to take me through all four growth gates for me to become who He wanted me to be. I would not have been able to see this pattern or learn these lessons without the brokenness of these years. I've finally learned not to be bent on *doing* more when God's focus is on my *being* more. It was a hard lesson, but worth learning. I believe it will be for you, too.

God's Pattern Repeated

When the pattern in Joseph's life became clear to me, I wondered, *Is this unique to Joseph, or is this* God's *pattern for all of us?* If it was God's game plan, it would be all over Scripture. So I started looking at the lives of people in the Bible who "grew up" in their faith and served God as effective leaders. I looked at the life of David, and there it was:

Winning Dependence: David became famous in the land when he relied on God to fight Goliath, but his dependence on God was a learned pattern in his life. When King Saul questioned whether David would be able to face the giant, David replied, "The LORD who rescued me from the paw of the lion and the paw of the bear will rescue me from the hand of this Philistine."[10]

Winning Within: David's dependence on God formed his character and made him a man after God's own heart. Even after Samuel had anointed David to be the next king of Israel, David showed patience, discipline, and respect as he waited upon God to elevate him to the throne. Twice David could have easily struck Saul down, and twice he spared him. And though it's true that David later stumbled and sinned against God and others, he always came back to God and put himself at God's mercy.

Winning with People: David's ability to win with people was clear. Crowds cheered for him. He won the heart of Jonathan, Saul's son, even though the king's heir should have seen him as a rival. He won over his mighty men and a small army of followers. And he gained people's loyalty by making it his practice to share the plunder after a battle (1 Samuel 30).

Winning Results: Finally, all these things put David in a place where he was able to get results. He grew as a warrior, mastering the sword and bow. He became a great leader and conqueror. He united the twelve tribes of Israel and brought peace to the land. He became a great and powerful king.

I looked at other biblical figures, and I found that every effective leader followed the same pattern:

Daniel...

Dependence: He prayed to God three times a day in Babylon.

Character: He chose to follow God instead of the king's edict to worship him.

Relationships: He won the respect of his companions, the king, and the court.

Results: King Nebuchadnezzar made him ruler of the province of Babylon.

Peter...

Dependence: After vacillating between *I can do anything* and *I can't do anything*, Peter finally learned to rely on the Holy Spirit after Pentecost.

Character: He preached the Gospel even when threatened with death, and was eventually martyred for his faith.

Relationships: He earned respect and became the leader of the church in Jerusalem.

Results: He preached and thousands believed; he led a spiritual revolution that eventually turned the Roman Empire upside down.

Paul...

Dependence: After his road to Damascus experience, he relied on Christ day by day, while being stoned, shipwrecked, flogged, persecuted, and, ultimately, executed.

Character: He learned to be content in all situations.

Relationships: Though not one of the original twelve, he became the most respected follower of Christ and greatest missionary in the world.

Results: He planted churches throughout the known world and wrote the definitive theological works upon which the Christian faith is built.

Every leader I looked at in Scripture who fulfilled his or her potential lived according to this pattern. I began to believe that this was what Paul was writing about in Romans 12 when he spoke about following God's pattern instead of the world's.

John's Perspective

I have seen this same pattern in the lives of godly leaders. And I have also experienced it in my life...

Dependence: When I was still in college, I began learning how to truly depend on God. Every day at lunchtime, I would walk to a spot behind the old block house and spend an hour with God.

I was excited to be headed into the ministry, but I understood that without God, the only things I would be able to do in life would be wood, hay, and stubble—things that will burn up at the end of the world, not things worthy of God.

Character: When I was in my second church, God dealt with my character. At that time, some ladies in my church had asked me to visit their brother in the hospital. For a week I would stop in his room and we'd chat about the Cincinnati Reds or some other unimportant topic.

Then one day when I was still at the hospital, I called home and Margaret said she had just gotten word that the man had died. I was shocked, because I had seen him just an hour before. And I realized that I had never shared my faith with him. For months I fell under conviction as God dealt with my character. I came to the point where I made a decision: I would make sharing my faith a lifelong priority. And whenever God prompted me to be His witness, I would.

Relationships: I've always been a people person, but that doesn't mean I've always done the right things relationally. One of the biggest relationship lessons I had to learn was with Margaret. Early in our marriage, I made it a point to win every argument. But I realized I was hurting her every time I did so. I had to learn to put her ahead of winning.

Results: When I started my career as a pastor, my lifetime goal was to lead a church of five hundred people. I had already achieved that in my mid-twenties. All I can say is this: God has allowed me to do more than I ever dreamed. I can never adequately show Him my gratitude.

The discovery of the four growth gates was a lightbulb moment for me. But as I processed all this information, I realized that I knew people of faith who valued all four of these areas yet still found their spiritual lives at a standstill. They were not experiencing life to the full! Why was that?

The answer is a profoundly simple insight that will literally change the way you live. It's the difference between hitting a home run and being called out. I've taught it to thousands of people in my congregation who would tell you, "Once you see it, you'll never see life the same." But before I took it public, I first taught it to my firstborn son, Josh. I'll share that process with you in the next chapter.

John's Application Guide

Discussion Questions

1. It can be said that there are three kinds of people:
   A. Those who have experienced brokenness and become bitter toward God.
   B. Those who have experienced brokenness and become dependent on God.
   C. Those who have not yet experienced brokenness.

   Which type of person are you? If you can become a mature Christian leader only by experiencing brokenness and dependence on God, are you willing to ask God for brokenness? Explain.

2. Prior to reading this chapter, what would you have identified as the key or keys to spiritual growth and maturity?
3. Kevin said he identified strongly with Joseph's story. Do you also identify with Joseph? If so, why? If not, with which biblical figure do you more readily identify? Explain.
4. Kevin asserted that all leaders who grow up in their faith and serve God effectively have had to win in the areas of dependence, character, relationships, and effectiveness. Can you think of someone from the Bible who clearly did not win in those four areas? How well did he or she serve God? Can you think of a historic Christian leader who finished well yet did not win in those four areas?

5. Do you believe any person can live a fulfilling and productive life while losing in one or more of the four areas? Explain.
6. Have you ever experienced a time with God that gave you great hope and high expectations for your life, only to be let down later by the way things turned out? If so, how did it impact you?
7. Which of the four areas do you find to be the greatest challenge to you personally? Why?
8. What are you willing to do to improve in that area?

Assignment

Set aside several blocks of time to do the following:

1. Goals and Plans: Spend some time thinking about your goals, hopes, and plans—past, present, and future. Reflect back on the goals and hopes of your youth. Then think about how your life has unfolded up to now. How differently have things turned out compared with what you had expected?

    Now think about your current hopes, dreams, and goals. Are you in a place where you are successfully accomplishing these things? Or do you feel more like you are struggling?

    Based on your observations, what might God be trying to teach you? What might He be trying to develop in you? What are your hopes? Write about them in your journal.

2. Biblical Models: Of all the people whose stories are recorded in the Bible, with whom do you identify most? In the next few days or weeks, read or reread the passages in Scripture that contain that person's story. Ask God to reveal His truths to you as you read. Try to discern the lessons that can be learned from his or her story and how God interacted with the person. Record your observations in your journal and spend time reflecting on them.

(Continued)

If you don't readily identify with a biblical figure or if you sense that your limited knowledge of the Bible may be preventing you from identifying with someone in it, put yourself on a biblical reading program. I recommend reading Genesis, Exodus, Luke, and Acts to start getting a grasp on the Bible relatively quickly. Those four books contain many of the stories of significant people in Scripture.

4

Parables, Baseball, and the Home Run Life

Understanding and living by the four growth gates of winning dependence, winning within, winning with others, and winning results was changing my life and my walk with God. Instead of merely expecting God to make life *easier*, I had a deep sense that God was growing me to make life *better*. Initially, that went against the grain for me. Like most people, I wanted a microwave quick-fix faith while God wanted to develop my maturity in the Crock-Pot of obedience.

John's Perspective

We live in a microwave culture that wants everything in an instant. That attitude often puts us out of step with God and how He works. God sees everything from an eternal perspective. Psalm 90:4 says, "A thousand years in your sight are like a day that has just gone by, or like a watch in the night."

Because God cares about who we are, not just what we do, He allows us the time we need to change. He wants to put us in the

(Continued)

Crock-Pot of change so that the changes we experience are deep and meaningful.

I tell people all the time that we don't need any more microwave leaders. I think it's also true that we don't need any more microwave Christians.

Put yourself in God's hands and trust Him to mold you into the person you were created to become, just as the potter works the clay. Then you will be ready for whatever God calls you to do.

As I grew, my hope for the future increased. My sense of peace in the present process of growth also helped me to relax and be less insecure. The Bible was coming alive as stories from the Old and New Testaments made more sense to me through the filter of what God had taught me. It was like the experience of buying a particular kind of car and then seeing it everywhere because you're looking for it.

The puzzle pieces of my life were coming together. But if I had stopped there, I'd have missed the profoundly simple realization that gave me insight on why most Christians live like non-believers. It was an idea capable of transforming our thinking and living, and I discovered it in a common game.

At that time, my oldest child, Josh, was turning eleven years old and about to enter middle school. While not every Christ follower is called to lead a church, all parents are called to lead their children. I was carrying a deep sense of inadequacy as a father, particularly when it came to transferring faith to my son. Of course he was attending church every week, and we had ongoing faith talks. At my direction, he was reading the Bible and praying. But I did not know how to give him the big picture of faith. How could I paint a clear picture of God's game plan for life? I think many parents struggle with this.

My sense of inadequacy was further intensified by my belief that we as parents are *not* here to raise children. Rather, I believe we are here to raise adults. The end goal of parenting is to raise emotionally, spiritually, and relationally whole adults who can make a competent contribution in their lives and career. They are only children for a short season, and in the time we have them, we can try to impress upon them the truths we embrace.

The truths I'd learned from the four growth gates in the life of Joseph were things I wanted to pass on, but I did not have a hook— a memorable angle—to make the ideas accessible to my son. What I needed was a parable. I needed a way to teach the truth of how to win in life and do it in such a way that a boy his age could easily grasp it, yet it would retain its depth and insight as he moved into manhood.

Parables were what Jesus used. In the Gospels, Jesus often compared spiritual truths to ordinary occurrences that everyone related to. For example, Jesus said...

> "The kingdom of heaven is like a man who sowed good seed in his field." (Matthew 13:24)
>
> "The kingdom of heaven is like a net that was let down into the lake and caught all kinds of fish." (Matthew 13:47)
>
> "The kingdom of heaven is like a landowner who went out early in the morning to hire workers for his vineyard." (Matthew 20:1)
>
> "The kingdom of heaven will be like ten virgins who took their lamps and went out to meet the bridegroom." (Matthew 25:1)
>
> "It [the kingdom of heaven] will be like a man going on a journey, who called his servants and entrusted his wealth to them." (Matthew 25:14)

Jesus's parables were about what was common to people in Israel during that time—farming, fishing, and manual labor. The illustration was usually simple, but the truth was complex, nuanced, and deep. No wonder Jesus was always saying, "He who has ears to hear, let him hear."

A Metaphor for Today

When I started searching for a metaphor, a modern-day parable, I discovered it in a game that every American child has seen and nearly all have played. I'm sure you've already figured out what it is: baseball. We all understand the basics of baseball. America's national pastime is deeply embedded in our culture. Six-year-olds play it in organized leagues. College athletes play at a high level. Pro athletes play in a multibillion-dollar industry. Middle-aged men and women way past their athletic prime spend nights and weekends on diamonds playing a variation called slow-pitch softball. Kids in cities grab a broom handle and use parked cars and manhole covers as bases. Even small children with only an inflatable rubber ball play kickball, which mimics baseball's rules. Today if Jesus were teaching people in America and He said, "The kingdom of God is like a game of baseball," people would be able to understand what He was trying to teach.

Inspired by baseball, I began teaching Josh about God's game plan for living, about how to get a home run life. And it worked! The baseball metaphor made the principles accessible and brought them to life. Then I started sharing it with friends and a business group I was mentoring at the time. The more I taught it, the better the analogy fit. I created a sermon series around it and taught it to my entire congregation. For more than a decade I've used it to help people pursue God and His life to the full, and now I want to teach it to you. You'll understand why baseball works so well when I get to the part about where most of us break down and mess up our lives—and how we can turn things around and follow God's pattern for a home run life.

Baseball Basics

Before I describe how the four growth gates relate to baseball, let me start by reviewing some of the basics of the game. No matter what level you're playing at—from sandlot stickball games all the way up to the World Series—some things are always true:

1. There are always four bases.
2. You score only when you cross home plate.
3. You must touch first, second, and third bases before crossing home plate.
4. You must run the bases in order.
5. If you miss a base, you're out.

Though there are many levels and variations of baseball, these five things never change. You don't start out with four bases in Little League and then move up to five bases in high school, six in college, seven in the minor leagues, and on up to eight in the big leagues. No, there are only four bases. And at every level, all the essential rules remain the same.

Using those baseball basics, you can overlay God's pattern for living and say that in life, there are really only four "bases," the four components we discovered in the life of Joseph. These are the things we must win before we can "score" according to God's game plan:

Home Plate—Winning Dependence
First Base—Winning Within
Second Base—Winning with Others
Third Base—Winning Results

No matter who you are or where you are in life, these are the four things you need to win. If you were to look at every self-help book, every spiritual formation guide, every life management manual, and every spoken sermon, you would find that the subjects they address would always fall into one of these four categories. They are as valid for a middle schooler, like Josh at that time, as they are for someone like me in middle age with a career and family.

The rules and the bases are always the same. The only thing that changes is the league of play. There are many leagues of play, each with its own skill level. But the four bases and the way a person scores are always the same. You have to cross home plate or you are out.

Let's take a closer look at each base and its corresponding value:

Home Plate—Winning Dependence

In baseball, players start and end at home plate. The goal of every batter is to connect with the ball and get around the bases. Keep doing that and you win. The same is true in God's game plan for life. It starts and ends with God. As you *connect* with Him, you grow in dependence on Him, just as Joseph did. The key word at home plate is Connect. It is at this base that we find *purpose* and *power.*

The ability to connect with your Creator changes everything. As you connect with your Heavenly Father, who is the author of life, you begin to understand who He is. He has eternally existed. He exists in spirit and has created other spiritual beings, His angels. He created the material world—everything in the universe—out of nothing. When He created mankind, including you, He did something totally radical: He wrapped a spiritual being inside a material body. As you learn more about God and about His perspective, you begin to realize that your purpose is bigger than life on earth. It has an eternal dimension. Your soul was created to live forever, and you will spend eternity either with or without God.

If your sense of purpose begins and ends with earthly living, you are missing God's intended plan and purpose for you. In His fatherly love for us, God seeks to help us see more and live larger than our years on earth. It's similar to the way we try to help our children gain a larger view of life than their immediate experiences. For example, my son Jadon, who is nine years old, can get so wrapped up in Legos that he thinks his bedroom and the toys in it are the beginning and end of the world. I want to prepare him for more than that in life.

Our connection with God begins on earth and extends into heaven. It is initiated when we say yes to Christ, but that is only the beginning if we live according to God's game plan. Our connection develops and grows as we pray, worship, read Scripture, fast, meditate, journal, serve, and give. Remember that Romans 12:1–2 tells us to offer ourselves to God as living sacrifices. In that way we conform not to the world but to God's plan, and as a result we will be able to discern God's will and purpose for our lives. So every act of worship serves to help us better connect with God. And the better connected we are, the greater our dependence. As we understand that we cannot pull off God's purpose with our power or use His power for our purpose, God gives us greater access to His power for His purpose. And that gives us direction and the ability to move on to the next base.

First Base—Winning Within

In baseball, the first sign of success is making it to first base. In the baseball analogy, first base represents Character. This is *the personal base*, the place where we must fight and win our internal battles, just as Joseph did.

When we come into a relationship with God, most of us are deeply impacted by the experience of His forgiveness. As we realize the magnitude of God's power, we start praying for Him to change things. Our prayers often sound something like this:

O God, please change my finances; I need more money. Please change my work; I need a better job. Please change my boss because she doesn't understand me. Please change my co-worker because he can be a jerk. Please change my spouse—I had no idea who I was marrying. Please change my kids. (They have a lot of my spouse in them.) And please change the economy and the country and...

But what is the very first thing God wants to use His power to change? Us! The changes God wants to see are *within* us, not *around* us. Our breakthrough comes when we realize that the first purpose of God's power is to change us from within by growing godly character.

If you don't settle home plate dependence on God, then you cannot tame your ego. You end up becoming your own god, and you lack the power to grow in character. This inability to be a person of character leads to other problems. It undermines others' ability to trust you and creates other breakdowns at home and work.

It takes character to manage ourselves, to do the morally right thing, to keep working when we're tired or discouraged, to resist temptation. We must deal with our emotions, direct our will, take charge of our thinking, and be responsible for our attitudes. How well you manage personal character determines how well you do life. John Maxwell says, "The development of character is at the heart of our development, not just as leaders, but as human beings...Unaddressed cracks in character only get deeper and more destructive with time."[1] The good news is that God wants to help us change and grow in the area of character. He wants to help us win within.

Second Base—Winning with Others

Every baseball player wants to make it to first—to get on base. But things usually don't get very exciting until a player arrives at second base. Why? Because that's where a player moves into scoring position.

In our analogy, second base is all about Community. That's why I call it the *people base*. If you can work with people and do well with them, that puts you into scoring position for life.

Life is designed to be an experience in community. When God made Adam, He created the individual. When He created Eve, he introduced community. God made it possible for us to do life together. But when sin entered the world, the beginning of relational breakdowns occurred. Adam and Eve's relationship became strained. Cain and Abel, the first two brothers, had an ugly falling-out leading to murder. And problems continued from there. If you read the Old Testament, though, you see that God often gave instructions designed to teach us to live in community and win relationships with others. For example, five of the Ten Commandments contain insights on how to treat and value others. Clearly God cares about relationships.

The New Testament reasserts the value God puts on people and relationships. Jesus Himself says that relationships with people are second only to our relationship with God. When asked what the greatest commandment was, He answered, " 'Love the Lord your God with all your heart and with all your soul and with all your mind.' This is the first and greatest commandment. And the second is like it: 'Love your neighbor as yourself.'"[2] In a mere twenty-four words, Jesus communicated the importance of winning dependence by loving God with all our heart, soul, and mind (home plate), winning within by loving ourselves (first base), and winning with others by loving our neighbor (second base). These things go together and build upon one another.

If we want to become the people we were created to be, to have a home run life to the full, to succeed as spiritual leaders, and to fulfill our purpose, we must learn to win the people base and work with others—at home with family, at work with employers and colleagues, in church with fellow believers, and in our communities with neighbors and those in need.

Third Base—Winning Results

The key word at third base is Competence. To be effective in life, we have to be able to get things done. That's why third base is called *the performance base*. Results really do matter. In a kids' T-ball game, the organizers may say that nobody's keeping score, but the players know who's winning. Everyone cares about results.

God also cares about them. He wants us to do our work with excellence. Even slaves were instructed, "Whatever you do, work at it with all your heart, as working for the Lord, not for human masters, since you know that you will receive an inheritance from the Lord as a reward."[3]

I believe the advice God gives to work hard and do it with excellence also applies to employees in today's work world (many of whom feel likes slaves some days). God wants us to win results—in whatever we do.

Christians tend to label the work we do within the church as "sacred" and the work outside it "secular." But God sees everything we do as worthy of His attention. God is the author of work. It was His big idea! We shouldn't forget that God assigned work to Adam and Eve in the Garden of Eden. And Joseph's "secular" work in Egypt was successful as a result of God's being with him—and served a sacred purpose at the same time. There is no dividing line. God enjoys seeing us perform with competence wherever we are.

If we are competent—going back to the baseball analogy—we touch third base and are ready to head back toward home plate, "scoring" by fulfilling the purpose God gave us when we connected with Him in the batter's box. That takes us full circle. And every time we come up to bat again, we get to repeat the process.

The four growth gates fit perfectly on a common baseball diamond like the one in tens of thousands of parks around the country. The parable is something that anyone can understand. It has value both in a

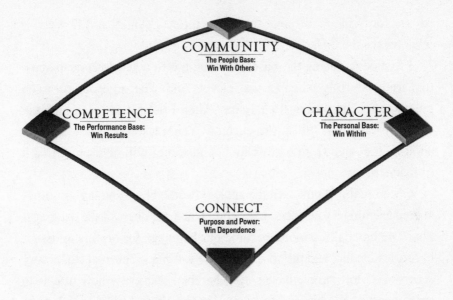

practical temporal sense and from an eternal perspective. To score in life and do things that matter, you need to win dependence on God at home plate, win character issues within at first base, win relationships in community at second base, win results at third base with competence, and return home completing God's purpose for your life. You have to win every base—and do it in the right order.

The Bases Are Our Common Language

As I taught the baseball diamond with each of the bases and what they represented, I could see that it was working for Josh. While the world would cheer him on for good grades, putting third-base competence first, my wife, Marcia, and I encouraged him to put character ahead of accomplishment. While his friends might say happiness can be found in relationships with girls, we encouraged him first to fight for his relationship with God at home plate. The order of priorities in God's pattern for living is different from our culture's. And that difference is what makes the difference.

I first began using the baseball metaphor to teach Josh deep spiritual truths starting when he was eleven, and it became our common language for discussing life's issues. Then I used it to teach and disciple my daughter, Julisa. I'm currently using it to teach Jake, who is about to graduate from high school. And soon I will begin teaching it to Jadon, my youngest.

Once I realized how well the analogy worked by using it with Josh, I started teaching it to leaders in the church and members of the congregation. The baseball diamond became our language for discussing issues in life, leadership, and the spiritual journey. It made spiritual truths very accessible. Most people have played baseball and know how it feels to strike out, to get a hit, and to score. Another thing I liked was that the parable describes an ongoing process. The game of baseball is filled with fresh starts and new beginnings. Every at-bat is a new experience. There are many games in every season. And if you become a dedicated player, you get many chances to step up to home plate and bat over a career.

Likewise, in the spiritual journey, every day is a fresh start, another chance to connect with God, win character battles, interact positively with people, and do work with excellence. And if we become dedicated to living life God's way and playing according to the pattern He desires, we get many at-bats over our lifetime, and we can score. We can have a home run life. Then why don't we? The secret lies in *how* we try to run the bases.

Where We Go Wrong

In baseball, do you know what they call it when you hit the ball and run to the wrong base? Little League! That's the only time it's funny.

When a four-year-old hits the ball off the tee and runs to the wrong base, everyone smiles. After all, the kid is just learning the game, and it's entertaining. The parents take videos and post them on YouTube. It's cute. But if you translate that picture into a spiritual truth, it can lead to one of life's greatest insights, a major-league breakthrough in understanding why people can acknowledge awareness of the four bases, yet end up losing out on life's dreams.

We run the bases backward!

In North America, performance is everything. How many people do you know who put career *first*? It's almost assumed, if not expected, that people will live for work and work to live. No wonder we see bumper stickers that say, THE ONE WHO DIES WITH THE MOST TOYS WINS. In a performance-driven society, you are elevated more by *what you do* and *what you earn* than by *who you are* on the inside. Career and material success become our core identity. It's so deep in the DNA of our culture that even many of us who become followers of Christ don't renew our minds as directed in Romans 12:2 when we surrender our lives to follow God. This pattern of the world is so ingrained, we are not aware that it's the world's way, not God's. So we conform to it out of habit and end up neglecting or ruining the most important things in life. We're trying to take a shortcut—to cheat—and we aren't even aware of it.

When we run to third base *first* as a life pattern, we cheat all the other bases. Under the pressure to perform, we cheat our marriage of the time, energy, and communication it needs to thrive—or even survive. Many people end up cheating morally because they have become relationally empty. How many have burned a marriage to build a career? How many have cheated on giving the time they needed to pour into their kids? For the sake of their careers, they neglect what's most important. By default or divorce, third-base runners end up estranged from the very people they brought into the world with the hope of helping to succeed. As a culture, we run to third base and then back to home plate and call it a home run, but the reality is that we lose out on our home life. The bigger dream gets cheated for something less important.

When we run to third base *first*, we cheat ourselves. We often sacrifice our health, violate our moral conscience, and accumulate cracks in our character that eventually undo the very success we tried to build on third base.

My son Jake has lived through the crash of two sports heroes in his eighteen years because they neglected their character while pursuing career success. When Jake was growing up, he was a football fan and loved to watch Michael Vick play for the Atlanta Falcons. Vick went to federal prison for dogfighting. Then in high school when Jake made golf his new sport, his hero was Tiger Woods. He cheated on his wife and broke up his family. How many more stories of moral failure do we need in the news to remind us that when you cheat at first base, you sabotage the dream of life? The biggest difference between Michael Vick or Tiger Woods and us is that our stories do not gain national attention. But the damage to our dreams can be just as great.

When we run to third base *first*, we also cheat our relationship with God. How many of us as followers of Jesus Christ are way too busy to read the Bible, pray, go to a worship service every seven days, or serve others to advance God's Kingdom on earth? We are consumed with the pattern of this world. And when the pressure comes, we offer an instant prayer seeking the will of God on the matter. But that runs contrary to what Romans 12:1–2 tells us. It says when we no longer conform to the pattern of this world, *then* we will be able to discern God's will, His good pleasing perfect purpose for our lives. How can we expect to know that when we're doing everything else our way?

Our world keeps calling it a home run when we race to third base

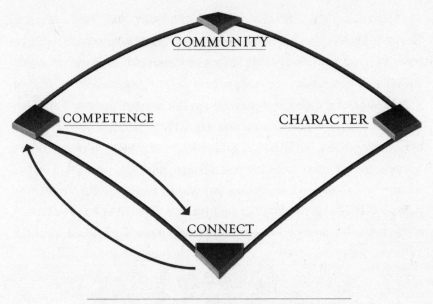

Some people run to third then back home

and back, but God calls it an out. And anyone who looks honestly at the long-term effects of living as a third-base runner also calls it an out. Running the bases backward doesn't work, because you lose out on the whole life dream. Everyone has similar dreams in life: We dream of success in a career, family, friends, self-respect, significance. Many people find success in one area, but they strike out in another. They gain success in career, but crash their marriage. They build their career, but break down their body. They fight to make time for family, and fail to find time for themselves. It's like trying to hold four beach balls underwater at the same time. One or more will always get away from you.

It's not that third base doesn't matter. It does. But the only way to win *all* of the bases is to run them in order. That is the issue. To live according to God's game plan, you must cover the bases in the order that makes sense according to God's values: home, first, second, third, and back to home. That's the only way to get a home run life.

This makes sense from a practical standpoint, too. Think about it: Business leaders are at their best when they are freed up emotionally by having a great marriage, solid kids, and a strong family. Business leadership is at its best when people are secure in their identity because of their relationship with their Creator, they are rock-solid in character, and they care more about others than about themselves. These kinds of people can develop trust, build teams, and work with a focus like few others because things are right in the rest of their life. Honestly, if you owned a business or led an organization, wouldn't you love to have a team of these kinds of people: humble faithful people with solid character, a stable home life, and good relationships who always get results at work?

John's Perspective

The first time Kevin shared the diamond with me and pointed out how most people run the bases the wrong way, putting third base first, I remember thinking, *This is our culture. This is where people live. This exposes where we get it wrong. This will help a lot of people.*

The temptation to run to third base first is very strong, especially in the business world. People do not pay for average. No one goes out of his way for mediocrity. Leaders don't want so-so teams. For that reason, people focus on third base first. But that's a short-term way of looking at things. Excellence over time is only sustainable when you put first things first.

The baseball diamond and the idea of running the bases the right way is very consistent with my understanding of leadership. When I teach the 5 Levels of Leadership, I explain that the first and lowest level of leadership is Position. For a Christian leader, where does everything begin? In your position in Christ. That corresponds to home plate. When you depend on God and connect with Him, you can be secure in who you are as a leader and open to what God wants to change in you. That leads to the character development that Kevin describes at first base.

The second level of leadership is Permission. This is where leaders develop relationships with others, and people begin to follow because they want to. That corresponds to second base on the baseball diamond.

The third level of leadership is Production. This is where people begin to follow because of what a leader does for the organization. This corresponds to third base—winning results.

Later in *Home Run*, Kevin will discuss making the circuit back to home plate and scoring. This corresponds to level four, which is People Development. When it comes to leadership, developing other people as leaders is how you score big. Kevin will also talk about moving up into higher leagues of play. That corresponds to level five: the Pinnacle. Just as only a few players make it to the hall of fame in Cooperstown, only a few leaders make it to the Pinnacle.

Other Wrong-Way Runners

Of course all the people who fail to follow God's game plan don't just run to third base. Some people run straight to second base, putting relationships first to the neglect of the other bases. In recent years, there has been a backlash against the performance focus of the baby boomers. As a result, younger generations have shifted their attention toward relationships, making them most important. You may hear people say things like,

Doing life with friends is most important.
My children are my life.
Family is everything.
When I get married, I'll be happy.

If you find yourself saying things like these, then you might be a second-base runner. You may be essentially running to second base and back home and calling it a score. Relationships, like career, are important. But they should never be first. God is always first. Going to second base *first* won't provide life to the full, either. People are fallible, and if you put all your hope in them, you will be disappointed. We are meant to live in community, but community isn't everything.

Are there such things as first-base-only runners? Yes. I believe many individuals in the early monastic movement fell into this pattern. It prompted them to disconnect from the world and enter the cloister. Some Christians still try to disconnect from the world and other people. That is a problem because Jesus calls His followers to make disciples of others,[4] and Scripture says that we cannot separate love for our fellow human beings from a genuine love for God.[5] So clearly, skipping second base and ignoring people isn't an option if we want to live life as God invites us to.

Look at different types of people, and you can see that many want to run the bases their own way, focusing on only one base or winning some bases but neglecting others entirely. For example, some politicians seem to care only about second base. Their entire focus is on winning voters. If they get reelected, they call it a win. Or look at some churches; they encourage people to worship God, work on character, and win relationships, but they neglect third base. They say, "You shouldn't run a church like a business," as if God didn't care about doing things with excellence.

There are no shortcuts in the spiritual journey. You cannot skip bases or do things your own way and still have a home run life—a life that's whole and full as Jesus promises. You have to hit every base and do it in order. What's tragic is that most people who've messed up their lives have done the opposite. They start off as third-base runners because they think their careers will give them all they want in life.

After a while, they realize that career achievement and material gain can be very hollow, and they finally recognize the importance of people. As a result, they run from third base to second, hoping to repair the relationships they've damaged. Often they do this in a second or even third marriage. They may also try to rebuild relationships with their alienated children. But often they find themselves incapable of healing or sustaining their relationships. Why? Key character issues are foundational to relationship building.

In an attempt to salvage their relationships, they finally start trying to overcome some of their character issues at first base. But most hit a wall, because it's something they can't win on their own. If you're over forty and you've tried to change ingrained character habits, you know what a challenge this can be—trying to change diet and exercise disciplines if you've never developed them, working to hold your tongue if you're used to saying whatever you feel, making an effort to have a positive attitude when you've experienced a lifetime of pessimism. In desperation, many people seek God to finally get help from Him.

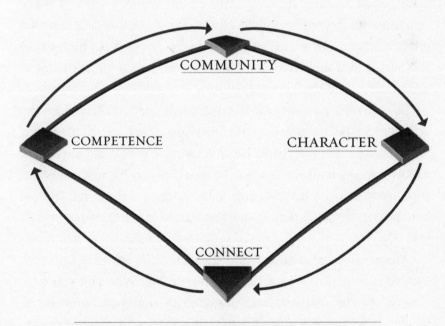

Some people run the whole diamond backwards

They've run the entire diamond backwards! They've moved to third-base competence, to second-base community, to first-base character, to home plate trying to connect with God. After a lifetime of running the wrong way, their lives are falling far short of what they expected, and they don't even know why. But the good news is that when they finally run into the arms of God, He has been waiting for them all along and is willing to help them. All they need to do is try to live according to His game plan.

A Change in Direction

Having been in ministry for more than thirty years, I've seen a lot of people like me who were running the bases of life the wrong way. One of those was Luis Ramos, a very successful businessperson. Like many people, he started life with big dreams: attending the U.S. Naval Academy and becoming a fighter pilot. But life happened, just as it does for all of us. He ended up getting married right out of high school and having kids. Instead of a naval career, he took a job in the insurance industry and was very successful.

But Luis felt an ever-growing discontent. He worked harder and earned more, but it didn't help. He knew something needed to change, so he quietly made a decision. He didn't want to restart his career—he had worked too hard for that—so he would restart the rest of his life. He'd take a do-over. He told his wife he wanted a divorce. Luis moved into the guest room of their home, and started to plan how they would split things up.

Around that same time, Luis attended 12Stone during a series on God's game plan for having a home run life. When Luis saw the diagram of the diamond and heard about third-base runners, he thought, *This is me. This is my life!* Luis realized he had been running the bases backwards his entire life, and he recognized the results.

Immediately he went to his wife, Roni, and told her, "Something's happened. I've made a terrible mistake. I want to change my life. I want you back."

It took many months for Roni to warm up to him, and it took years for him to re-earn her trust. But Luis persisted. And more important, he changed the way he lived. He turned his focus from the pursuit of career to the pursuit of God, and he began running the bases the right way. It changed his relationship with God, built his character, and saved his marriage.

What about his job? He had to sacrifice it for his family, right? No. After he put it where it belonged—after God, his integrity, and his family—it became even better than it was before.

"I had been throwing my life away," he says. "When I was chasing material stuff, it came hard. It was all-consuming. My entire focus was on working and earning. I spent untold hours at the office. I was trading everything for it. I said it was for my family, but that was a lie. Once I started running the bases the right way, I changed my hours and the time in the office. I wasn't forfeiting everything for my career. What's ironic is that I became much more successful materially."

I have to admit that I started my career running the bases the wrong way. I put my entire focus on achieving the vision—just as Joseph did. I had to learn to turn to God first and depend on Him, allowing Him to build character in me, and enabling me to repair and build my relationship with my family and others. That was the real work God wanted to do in me. Then and only then was I able to win at third base and fulfill my purpose by returning to home plate for a "score." When I started running the bases the right way after more than thirty-five years of life and almost two decades of Christian leadership, I was finally practicing Romans 12:2. I wasn't conforming any longer to the pattern of this world, but being transformed by the renewing of my mind. As a result, I was able to test and approve what God's will was—His good, pleasing, and perfect will.

John's Perspective

In the previous chapter, I gave you a definition of *success* that applies to everyone. Now I want to give you another definition. This is one that I believe applies to me: Success is having those closest to me love and respect me the most. Why do I say that? Because it's a reminder to me to take care of home plate and first base every day of my life. If I don't remain close to God and look after my character, I may do things that will damage my relationships with my wife, Margaret, my children and their spouses, and my five grandchildren.

Which Way Are You Going to Run?

What kind of base runner have you been in your life? Have you been unknowingly conforming to the pattern of this world, running the bases backwards? Or have you been skipping bases and calling it a score? The good news is you can change. But you must be willing to live God's way. That is going to take a process. It's one thing to *understand* baseball and to watch a game. It takes much more effort to actually *play* baseball and succeed, especially at a higher level. Hitting a ninety-mile-an-hour fastball is no easy task. Hitting a curveball is even harder. You have to work your way up to it. You have to start in a league that matches your skill, abilities, and experience. You have to learn a lot before you are able to play at a higher level. It takes time and work.

The remaining chapters in this book are designed to help you learn how to win each base and do so in the right order. We want to help you run the bases the right way and have a home run life by living out God's dream for you. The next four chapters will explain the intricacies of the bases and how to win them. We will coach you so that you can improve your game. We will continue to include discussion questions and activities at the end of each chapter. You can think of them as batting practice.

John's Perspective

A high school home run hitter received an invitation to spring training from a major-league team. After the first week, he emailed home to say, "Dear Mom, leading all batters. These pitchers are not so tough." The next week he boasted, "Now hitting .500 and it looks like I will be starting in the infield." However, the third week, he wrote, "They started throwing curveballs today. Will be home tomorrow."

Don't allow the curveballs of life to take you out of the game. Hang in there and keep training. You can receive God's best for you, fulfill your purpose, and have a home run life if you are willing to learn to run the bases of life the right way.

As you proceed, remember this. The spiritual journey, like baseball, is not meant to be a single at-bat. It represents an entire career. You'll get many chances to come up to the plate, and it doesn't matter how many times in the past you've struck out. Once you've accepted Jesus, you're on God's team; you wear His jersey. So accept God's invitation to get into the game and learn under His coaching, and when you get into the game, play to win.

John's Application Guide

Discussion Questions

1. What is your personal experience with the game of baseball? What form did you play: hardball, softball, kickball? Overall, would you say your experience has been positive or negative?
2. In your life, what "base" have you focused most of your time and energy on winning: home (winning with God), first (winning within), second (winning with others), or third

(Continued)

(winning results)? How has that focus impacted your life positively? How has it impacted it negatively?

3. What base have you neglected the most? How has that impacted your life?

4. Do you agree that it's important to run the bases in the order suggested in the chapter? Explain why or why not.

5. How might your life change if you followed the pattern suggested in the chapter?

6. What immediate step are you willing to take to change the way you do life?

Assignment

Set aside at least several hours and possibly an entire day to get away and assess the way you've been living your life. Write a list of what's most important in your life. Then assess how you have been ordering your priorities based on how much focus, time, effort, and money you've dedicated to them. After that, look at each priority and designate which base it falls under. Spend time in prayer talking to God about what you discover, and listening to sense His response.

5

Home Plate: How to Win with God

When a major-league baseball player steps up to home plate in a game, he knows what he is supposed to do. Get a hit. If he gets a hit, he gets on base, and that will give him an opportunity to score. That's the reason good players spend so much time practicing their batting. They work on their stance. They perfect their swing. They learn to

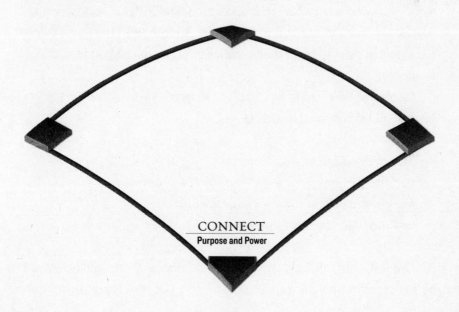

CONNECT
Purpose and Power

read pitches. They work hard at home plate. Why? Because they need to connect with the ball. If they don't, they have no hope for a home run.

In life, as in baseball, everything starts and ends with home plate. More to the point, everything starts and ends with God. To have the life we want, we need to connect with God. When we don't, we often get ourselves into trouble.

God Helps Those Who Help Themselves—Really?

The willful human desire to be independent and go our own way is as old as the Garden of Eden. And it has continued down through humankind. One of the best examples in Scripture of someone who wanted God's blessing while going his own way was Jacob, the son of Isaac (and father of Joseph). Jacob was a man who really wanted to succeed in life. His name can be translated as "heel catcher" or "trickster." But a better way to express it might be "go-getter."[1] Jacob was somebody who went after what he wanted, and his goal was to be successful financially—to win in his career, so to speak. He was a third-base runner. And it didn't much matter to him what he had to sacrifice to succeed.

Jacob was destined to be a leader. Scripture says that before he was born, God told his mother, Rebekah,

Two nations are in your womb,
and two peoples from within you will be separated;
one people will be stronger than the other,
and the older will serve the younger.[2]

Did Rebekah tell Jacob that he would father a nation and be served by his older brother? Scripture doesn't say. But it's certain that Jacob was doing everything he could to get ahead—even if it meant cutting corners in his character and burning relationships. He conned Esau out of his birthright, getting the older brother to trade it for a bowl of lentil stew. Then later Jacob tricked his father into giving him Esau's blessing.

Why would Jacob work so hard to have those two things? Because the person who received the birthright of the first son and got his father's blessing would be the recipient of God's favor. He would be entitled to the majority of the family's wealth. And he would have the place of power and authority in the family when Isaac died. Jacob was willing to compromise his integrity and risk alienating his family to get what he wanted. In other words, he wanted God's power, but for his own purpose.

I think that's the way many of us approach life. We go after what we want or what we think should be ours, and we hope God will bless us and help us along the way. *God, please give me this*, or *God, help me to do that*, we ask. We ask God to bless what we're doing instead of trying to do what God's blessing. I know that's what I did when I started 12Stone Church. God had given me the vision, so I went after it *my* way and assumed God would bless it. But God was more interested in who I *became* than in what I *did*. That was true for Jacob as well. It's also true for you.

Let's Make a Deal

When people don't connect with God, they are more likely to compromise their character at first base. Once they've done that, it's just another small step to do damage to their relationships at second base. That was true for Jacob. He lied to his father and his brother Esau. Jacob's brother was so enraged that he decided he'd rather kill Jacob than allow him to move ahead of him in the family. In response, Jacob took flight. He headed to his uncle Laban's house. But along the way, Jacob had a heavenly vision, in which God said to him,

> I am the LORD, the God of your father Abraham and the God of Isaac. I will give you and your descendants the land on which you are lying. Your descendants will be like the dust of the earth, and you will spread out to the west and to the east, to the north and to the south. All peoples on earth will be blessed through you and your offspring. I am with you and will watch over you wherever you go, and I will bring you back to this land. I will not leave you until I have done what I have promised you.[3]

Wow! What a promise. God said He'd deliver on everything He'd promised to Abraham, Jacob's grandfather, and Jacob would be the recipient. It was probably more than even Jacob the go-getter could have ever imagined.

What was Jacob's response?

> *If* God will be with me and will watch over me on this journey I am taking *and* will give me food to eat and clothes to wear so that I return safely to my father's household, *then* the LORD will be my God. [emphasis added][4]

That sounds like a pretty weak response. But let's not condemn Jacob too quickly. Others with the benefit of hindsight could look at us and say that our responses to Christ's promises of life to the full are similarly weak. Jesus says that if we seek His kingdom first, we'll have everything else we'll need. Yet we still pursue our own agendas.

To use an analogy, think of life as a pie. When we become Christians, we say, "Okay, God. Thank you for saving my life," and we assign God a slice of life's pie. As God invites us to grow, we see that process as giving God an increasingly bigger piece of our pie. Maybe we started at 5 percent and we increase it to 10 percent or even 25.

What's wrong with that perspective? It looks at life in slices or compartments. We have our work slice, our marriage slice, our family slice, our finance slice, our hobby slice, our religious slice. But that's not how God looks at it. God is saying, "No, no, no. I don't want a sliver of 'your' pie. I'm not a slice of your life separate from the rest of it. I'm the crust! I hold everything together. Give your whole life to me. I undergird everything: your work, marriage, family, finances, hobbies—all of it. This is part of the process of renewing your mind. This is what leads to a transformed life."

You get the sense that when Jacob received the vision, he was still scheming with God. He offered up a slice of his pie only if God gave him everything he wanted. In other words, he was saying, "Follow my agenda, God, and it's a deal." In those moments, Jacob's goal never changed. He still wanted success. He worked for his uncle in order to make his fortune. When he saw Rachel and fell in love with her, he was only too glad to do more work to get her.

It's true that Jacob succeeded financially, but he did so in the midst of strife. He made a mess of his relationships, which you can see from his dysfunctional family, made up of an alienated brother, a deceitful father-in-law, jealous wives, competing concubines, angry brothers-in-law, and offspring who engaged in world-class sibling rivalry. (His sons were the jealous brothers who sold Joseph into slavery.) Jacob made his fortune, but he paid for it in other ways. And when he was finally ready to go back home after twenty-two years of work, he felt he had to sneak away in the middle of the night. He was still cutting corners.

Wrestling Match

As you read Jacob's story, you think he's never going to change. He's always working an angle. He's always trying to get ahead in an under-handed way. He works the system and cuts corners. He wheels and deals. Sometimes he gets taken by the person he's dealing with, as he did when Laban substituted Leah for Rebecca on his wedding night. Other times he is the one who gets the upper hand, as he did with old Isaac and later with Laban and the herds.

But then something happened to Jacob that changed everything for him. On his way back to his homeland as he faced the possibility that Esau and his four hundred men might kill him and all of his family the next morning, Jacob found himself in a wrestling match. It was the first time Jacob met God on God's terms. Genesis 32:24–30 says,

> So Jacob was left alone, and a man wrestled with him till daybreak. When the man saw that he could not overpower him, he touched the socket of Jacob's hip so that his hip was wrenched as he wrestled with the man. Then the man said, "Let me go, for it is daybreak."
>
> But Jacob replied, "I will not let you go unless you bless me."
>
> The man asked him, "What is your name?"

Have you ever read this story and wondered why this manifesta-tion or representative of God would ask Jacob his name? Certainly He knew the answer. So we have to conclude that He wasn't asking for information.

What if He was asking for a confession? The last time Jacob was asked that question, his answer was a lie: "I am Esau."[5] This time— probably for the first time in his life—Jacob was honest with himself and with God:

"Jacob," he answered.

Then the man said, "Your name will no longer be Jacob, but Israel, because you have struggled with God and with humans and have overcome."

Jacob said, "Please tell me your name."

But he replied, "Why do you ask my name?" Then he blessed him there.

So Jacob called the place Peniel, saying, "It is because I saw God face to face, and yet my life was spared."

All his life prior to that night, Jacob had lived his own way, pretending to be someone other than who he actually was, and keeping God safely at a distance. Jacob was always glad to receive God's favor if God would give it (like us!), but he didn't want God to get hold of him and interrupt his agenda. On this night, God put Jacob in his place—powerless and wholly dependent on God. With the slightest touch, God crippled Jacob for life. With a word God could have destroyed him. In that moment, Jacob finally understood that God didn't owe him. He *owned* him. Jacob recognized his dependence on God. And when God asked him who he was, Jacob was no longer pretending to be Esau or anyone else. He confessed who he was. The trickster. The guy who took shortcuts. In today's parlance, the man who always neglected first base and ran to third. And even though God had no reason to do so, He blessed Jacob and gave him a new identity.

What if that is God's intention with you and me? What if He wants us to stop pretending to be someone we're not? We are not in control of our lives. We are not capable of becoming the person God created us to be on our own. We do not have it all together. We cannot stay on our own agenda and be blessed by God. We cannot live life to the full our way.

John's Perspective

When I was a young leader, I thought I had to be someone I wasn't. Because I was only twenty-two years old trying to lead people in their thirties, forties, and fifties, I thought I had to have all the answers. I thought I had to come across as really smart, especially when I was preaching. So what did I do? I'm embarrassed to say that I wore glasses even though I didn't need them. How foolish was that?

I knew that I wanted to become a good speaker, to become a communicator. But when I first started speaking, I was very average. I tried a lot of things, many of which were not really me. It took me eight years to learn how to be myself in front of an audience. And that's when God was finally able to start using me.

My friend Joyce Meyer says, "God will help you be all you can be—all you were originally designed to be. But He will never permit you to be successful at becoming someone else." How do you come to understand who God made you to be? Connect with Him and learn to depend on Him.

All of Jacob's life, he had been defensive. He had kept God at a distance and done his own thing. In his wrestling, he finally became dependent. Frederick Buechner, in *The Magnificent Defeat*, writes,

Power, success, happiness, as the world knows them, are his who will fight for them hard enough; but peace, love, joy, are only from God. And God is the enemy whom Jacob fought there by the river, of course, and whom in one way or another we all of us fight—God, the beloved enemy. Our enemy because, before giving us everything, he demands of us everything; before giving us life, he demands our lives—our selves, our wills, our treasure.[6]

It took Jacob twenty years to confess who he was before God and finally experience a breakthrough. By giving himself up to God, he discovered that the blessing he received was for God's glory, not just his own personal gain.

How long will it take you to submit to God? What is stopping you from declaring your dependence on Him? God can't bless who you want to be. He can only bless who He created you to be. If you want life to the full, you must live out His purpose with His power. Anything else falls short.

How Will You Live?

You cannot live life to the full without knowing God's purpose for your life and receiving His power to fulfill it. Is that how you are living? Most people don't really think about it in those terms. They just live. But when it comes right down to it, there are really only four ways that people approach life. Which one are you living?

Our Purpose with Our Power—The Empty Life

Everyone begins life trying to do his own thing under his own power. The majority of people in this world still fall into this category. People search for some kind of purpose wherever they can find it, and they pursue it however they can. Human beings can accomplish a lot under this scenario—and have. They can gain wealth, build empires, create technological marvels, pursue relationships—but their actions ultimately bring a sense of emptiness. Mathematician and philosopher Blaise Pascal observed, "There is a God shaped vacuum in the heart of every man which cannot be filled by any created thing, but only by God, the Creator, made known through Jesus." Most people who are honest with themselves will admit the emptiness they feel, though many would not be able to identify the reason for it.

King Solomon is said to be one of the greatest men who ever lived. He had it all. He sat on a royal throne. He possessed untold wealth. He ruled an empire. He built great cities. He had as many wives and concubines as his heart desired. He possessed great knowledge and is said to have been the wisest man who ever lived. Yet in Ecclesiastes he wrote that all human pursuits without God are meaningless vanities, leading to emptiness. Only a life lived for God has meaning. He wrote, "To the person who pleases him, God gives wisdom, knowledge and happiness."[7]

Our culture commends those persons who live life on their own terms. The old song celebrates that I did it my way. Yet the reality is that people who live without God experience emptiness and sorrow at the end of their lives. If we do not know God, we cannot be expected to do anything other than follow our own purpose using our own power. That's why God offers us a way out.

Our Purpose with God's Power—The Unfulfilled Life

Many of the people who call themselves Christians spend most of their lives following their own purpose and hoping that God will give them the power to succeed. They are like Jacob. They have an encounter with God (as Jacob did in Bethel on his way to Laban's house), but they don't significantly change the direction of their life in response to it. They stay on their own agenda and keep doing what they've always done, yet they ask God to bless it. That doesn't work.

If you have come to Christ for salvation but you think your life will stay on the same course as before you met Him, your expectations are wrong. If you resist changing your agenda, you won't have the full life you desire. You will always feel unfulfilled.

If the God you follow is manageable, then you are following the god you created, not the God who created you. If you've ever said, "I don't believe in a God who would _____ [fill in the blank] because *my* God would never do that," then you've created a god you can control and who exists according to your standards. In other words, *you* are really your own God.

If you want to fulfill God's purpose for you, then like Jacob you need to let go of the god you have created and grab on to the God who created you. Interaction with the real God is always dangerous. It's never comfortable, easy, and safe. If you're not being corrected, if you're not being made uncomfortable, if your beliefs, habits, and practices are not being regularly challenged, then you are not connected to God and wrestling with Him. And you won't have the home run life you desire.

God's Purpose with Our Power—The Frustrated Life

Not everyone has a type A personality, holding on to their own agenda and expecting God to bless it. Some people are very willing to hand themselves over to God and let God direct them. However, many of these people don't seem to have a home run life, either. While they may have some sense of what direction God wants them to take, they appear to be powerless to follow through. They don't get anywhere. Their lives are like that of Paul, described in Romans:

> I do not understand what I do. For what I want to do I do not do, but what I hate I do...For I have the desire to do what is good, but I cannot carry it out. For I do not do the good I want to do, but the evil I do not want to do—this I keep on doing.[8]

To have a sense of what you are to do—but to be powerless to fulfill it—is very frustrating. This seems to be where another large number of believers find themselves.

God's Purpose with His Power—The Full Life

What if the only way to live life to the full, to have a home run life, is to pursue God's purpose for you *and* to tap into His power to fulfill it? What if the way to do that is to be honest with yourself, depend on God, connect with Him, and *stay* connected with Him?

That sounds simple. And it is simple—in concept. It's easy to understand, but really hard to do. In fact, staying connected to God is so difficult that most people give up trying to do it and live without power, purpose, or both.

If that describes you, don't lose heart. Your life doesn't have to be that way. You can learn how to connect with God—and stay connected with Him so that you can stay in the game, discover your purpose, tap into God's power, and have a home run life.

John's Perspective

Knowing God's purpose for your life and connecting with His power to accomplish that purpose is something you should expect to be revealed over the course of your life, not all at once. Early on, sometimes the best you can do is go in the *direction* God indicates and see how things unfold. It's similar to driving at night. Your car's headlights show you only so much of the road ahead of you. How do you see more? Keep driving. The longer you stay on course according to God's direction, the more will be revealed and the more you will understand.

How Do You Stay Connected to God?

Most people find it relatively easy to connect with God right after they accept Christ, but more difficult to stay connected later. Why is that?

In the beginning, God does all the work. It starts with the fact that God has already sent His Son to die for our sins so that we might have eternal life. That is His gift to us. We don't deserve it, and we can't earn it. All we have to do is confess our sin and accept God's offer of life through faith. It's very similar to the way God treated Jacob the first time at Bethel. Jacob does nothing to hear from God. As Jacob sleeps, God appears and says He will bless him and be with him. All Jacob has to do is accept.

However, God doesn't necessarily make it easy for us to *stay* connected to Him. To do that, we have to work at it, just as Jacob did the second time he encountered God. Jacob had to wrestle with God all night to receive His blessing. Jacob hung on for dear life, finally having an idea about how valuable God's favor and blessing was. He didn't want to miss it, and he finally realized it was worth fighting for. That's quite a contrast to his earlier conditional response.

If we want a deeper faith and a fuller life, we have to strive for it. God made it clear that He expects us to chase Him. We are to ask, seek, and knock in active prayer and pursuit of God.[9] We often don't want to make the effort to do that. Most of us would prefer to be caught by God, but that is a lazy way to approach faith. To grow up, we must pursue God. And the good news is that He promises He will connect with us if we do that. The book of James says that if we draw near to God, He will draw near to us.[10]

God invites everyone to become a major-league player in His Kingdom. Unfortunately, when many find the task to be difficult, they become spectators instead. They walk off the field of play and sit in the stands, becoming mere fans of faith—or they become critics. If that has happened to you, get out of your seat, pick up your bat, and get back into the game.

Winning with God—In Leagues of Play

If you want to win with God by connecting with Him—and continuing to connect with Him all the days of your life—you must be willing not only to work at it, but also to reset your expectations. To help with that, let's return to the baseball analogy.

What's a good batting average in baseball? A player can make it professionally in Major League Baseball (MLB) by consistently batting .250. That means he gets a hit in one of four at-bats. If he can bat .333—connecting with the ball and getting on base one time in three—he's considered a great hitter. If he does that for a career, he would probably end up in the hall of fame.

Why bring this up? Because in the faith journey, even the most dedicated and consistent believers don't *feel* connected all the time. Our early encounters with God can be so overwhelmingly positive and palpable to us that we expect them to *feel* that way all the time. If we don't *feel* emotionally overwhelmed, we think we aren't connected to God. But that's not a realistic expectation. It would be like expecting to bat 1.000 in professional baseball. It's never been done.

So how do you know if you're connecting with God? Our answer is this: Are you *currently* working at it? Are you currently expressing your love to God? Are you *obeying* Him in the moment? Are you trying your best *today*—this minute? That's what Jesus was talking about when he admonished us to stay *in the vine*—to stay connected to Him continually.[11] But that doesn't mean we will *feel* connected all the time. And just like a vine, we experience times when we grow rapidly and times when we grow very slowly. We have seasons when we produce lots of fruit, and we have seasons when we are actually being prepared to produce and our growth may not be visible. As believers we should expect to experience ups and downs, highs and lows, vitality and fatigue. The only things we have control over are our intentions and effort *today*.

If you reset your expectations and understand that *daily intentionality* is the key to connecting with God, then the next thing you need to figure out is *how* to pursue God intentionally. To do that, let's return to the baseball analogy and think of trying to connect with God according to one of three "levels of play."

Amateur League—Learning God's Principles and Obeying

When most people make a decision to accept God's gift of Christ, they want to jump right into the game. That's good. If they've been highly successful in a career, they expect to jump into the faith journey at the same level they've enjoyed in their career. That's unrealistic. Would someone who has never played baseball expect to step into the pros? Of course not. Think about this. Michael Jordan, arguably the greatest basketball player of all time, retired from the NBA to play baseball. When he did, was he able to play on a major-league team? No. How about a AAA team? Nope. He never even made it past AA. And he was a world-class athlete!

In the spiritual journey, everyone starts at an amateur level. Everyone has to start at the lowest level and work his or her way up to higher leagues of play. And there are no walks, no free passes. But we can't let that discourage us from getting into the game.

If you have little experience with God and the spiritual journey, you need to start by getting to know God: His character, His thinking, how He interacts with people. You grow as you obey and follow through on what God reveals as His truth. How do you do that? Primarily by reading the Bible, God's words to us. When you are in phase one of your spiritual journey—as an amateur—you might want to spend 60 percent of your connect time with God reading the Bible and 40 percent of your time talking with God in prayer. And stay connected to your home church. It's likely they have basic training in the Bible and prayer that can help you get started.

To be blunt, this is where the breakdown is for most believers. They don't know the Bible. They don't know the stories of God's interaction with human beings. They don't know God's nature and His character. They don't know the principles outlined in Scriptures that reveal God's game plan for living and provide wisdom for life to the full.

If you don't have much experience reading the Bible, put yourself on some kind of plan where you read Scripture every day. If the thought of tackling the whole Bible is intimidating to you, start by reading Genesis, Exodus, Luke, and Acts. Those books contain many of the core stories of the early Hebrews, the life of Christ, and the start of the church. Once you've read those four books, then read the New Testament in its entirety. If you are unfamiliar with how to benefit from the reading, then read a chapter or two and ask these questions:

- **What did I read?** What is the story? Who are the people involved? What events occurred?
- **What can I learn about God's nature?** What is one thing the passage teaches me about God's nature? What is God like? What is His character?
- **What can I learn about human nature?** What one thing does the passage reveal about people? In what ways am I like the people in the passage?
- **What do I need to do to obey?** What one value or truth has been revealed to me? Is there something I should stop doing or start doing?

> ### John's Perspective
>
> Several years ago, Kevin did a sermon series called "Genesis to Revelation" offering an overview of the entire Bible that thousands of people have found helpful. It puts the major events of the Bible into perspective. You can listen to it for free on iTunes or 12Stone's website. It will help you improve your play at this level.

At the same time, start praying regularly. You might want to use the familiar ACTS model. It's simple but effective. Divide your prayer time into four parts:

Adoration: Reflect on one facet of God's character and express your love and adoration for who He is.

Confession: Admit where you've sinned since the last time you prayed, and ask God's forgiveness.

Thanks: Reflect on the good in your life and give God thanks for what He is doing. Gratitude keeps us in the vine as we pay attention to God's kindness.

Stuff: Ask God to give you what you need in every area of life: work, marriage, parenting, finances, and so on. Our Heavenly Father wants us to come to Him with our hopes and dreams, asking Him to do something huge in our lives.

It's pretty simple and straightforward. A friend of mine started using ACTS in a version called "Eight Minutes with God," spending two minutes on each prayer area. When he first started using it, two minutes felt *really* long. Now he can't imagine praying for only eight minutes.

Reading Scripture and praying during the "amateur" phase of the journey is like taking batting practice. In baseball, you're learning how to swing the bat and connect with the ball. In the spiritual journey, you're learning how to communicate and connect with God. Just like swinging a bat for the first time, it feels awkward and unnatural. You have to learn the fundamentals; otherwise you'll never be a candidate to move up to a higher league of play.

The other key part of this first phase of connecting with God is obeying Him. Jesus said, "Anyone who loves me will obey my teaching. My Father will love them, and we will come to them and make our home with them. Anyone who does not love me will not obey my teaching. These words you hear are not my own; they belong to the Father who sent me."[12] As we learn more about God, we discover more about ourselves that needs to change. The more we make the changes and corrections that God desires, the closer we are able to come to Him. The more dependent on God we realize we really are, the more He reveals Himself to us.

There's not a lot of fanfare for working hard at the amateur-league level. And the hardest part is being willing to change. As human beings, we have an unpleasant tendency to excuse our own sin, believing that God understands our "special circumstances." But the truth is that sin is sin. If you're having sex outside of marriage or taking something that doesn't belong to you or slandering another person, your difficulties won't excuse you.

When you learn one of God's principles and realize you are violating it, don't try to suppress the conviction you feel. *Pay attention to it!* God is connecting with you, so don't cut Him off. Realize that if you submit to God, He has more for you. He wants you to have a full life, and there are many things God cannot bless. He cannot bless sin.

Living in sin and asking God to bless it is like driving on the wrong side of the road and asking God to protect you. At some point, you're going to have a collision that brings loss, pain, and sorrow to yourself and others. The only proper response when you realize you're on the wrong side of the road is to change and do things God's way. Ask for

His forgiveness and favor, and depend on Him as you make adjustments to your life. Following through on this can turn your life upside down. It can be very uncomfortable. It can be scary. But you can't improve your life without changing it.

As you step out into these scary and difficult places, try to remember that God can take what others mean for harm and turn it to good, as He did with the actions of Joseph's brothers. Romans 8:28 says, "And we know that in all things God works for the good of those who love him, who have been called according to his purpose." That also applies to you. Just as it all worked for the good in Joseph's life, it can work for good in yours. It may take years, but if you submit to God, He will fulfill His purpose, and it will be good.

Minor League—Leaning into God's Prompts

If you are a follower of Jesus, you are not doing life alone. God is *in* you. You have the power of the Holy Spirit because you are "in the vine."[13] As you pray and read the Bible, you are actively engaging the kingdom of God on earth. Because of that, you will experience prompts from the Holy Spirit, not only as you pray, but as you do life. My friend Sam Chand calls this a "pinch" from God. Whatever you choose to call it, you need to recognize that it is a moment of supernatural awareness when God is asking you to do or say something that has kingdom value.

I've had these Holy Spirit prompts at work, while driving, during conversations, while enjoying a hobby, and during a church service. They are a good reminder that everything we do can be sacred. Ephesians 2:10 states, "For we are God's handiwork, created in Christ Jesus to do good works, which God prepared in advance for us to do." Life is not without meaning. God has work for us to do—which He has planned for us in advance—if only we are willing to connect with Him, depend on Him, and allow Him to empower us to do it.

These prompts have challenged my character in traffic when I sensed that I should slow down, not be so self-absorbed, and let a driver get in front of me. They have encouraged my marriage when I realized I should apologize, hold my tongue, or get up to serve my wife. Some prompts have caused me to perform a simple act of kindness for someone. For example, once while at Steak 'n Shake restaurant, my son and I were enjoying a late-night celebration after his band concert. Our waitress was a vibrant young lady in her early twenties. In the course of our meal, we learned that she was tired after spending all morning attending classes in community college, all afternoon taking care of her seventeen-month-old child (she was a single mom), and all evening working a shift until midnight. Even under those circumstances, she served with a smile and was customer-focused.

As we prepared to leave, I got a prompt: Lay down a big tip. Years before, God had prompted me to keep a twenty- and later a hundred-dollar bill in my wallet so that I'd be ready anytime He prompted me. We paid the tab, placed the hundred-dollar bill on the table, and walked out. Through the window as we headed to our car, we saw her stop at the table, turn in shock, run to the register (perhaps to see if it was a mistake), and then break down when she realized it was just to bless her.

We got in the car and my son said, "That was cool!" And it was, for we are God's players to be a force for God and for good in the world around us. One of the most powerful ways God proves His presence and love for others is through us. Being sensitive to God's prompts, along with praying and learning Scripture, is a way to go to the next league in your walk with God.

We have encouraged this in our congregation and have heard thousands of stories of God prompts and God moments for the good of others. One 12Stone member drove up to a Chick-fil-A restaurant and bought the meal for the car behind her. The expense turned out to be a sandwich and water. That didn't cost her too much. The following week she repeated the act. "I'd like to buy the meal for the car behind me," she said. "Here's my card, just run it." When she got the bill, it turned out to be $56. She was stunned because that was fifty bucks she didn't have. But then the next day she received a check in the mail from her doctor's office saying she had overpaid. Enclosed was a check for $50. I'm not saying you'll receive checks when you give, but it sure encouraged this 12Stone member to pay attention to prompts.

Another one of the positive things that happens at the minor-league level is that you begin to learn more about your purpose. When many Christians begin their faith journey with God, they understand for the first time that life can have purpose and deep meaning. But then they often expect God to lay out the entire picture for their lives in one fell swoop at the beginning of the journey. God doesn't usually do that. Even Joseph did not know what his vision meant when he was seventeen years old.

If God wants you to know some things early about His will for you, as he did for me in my call to ministry at age sixteen, then He will let you know. Meanwhile, you can begin by pursuing the universal purpose He has for everyone who calls him Lord. Jesus expressed it when asked about the greatest commandment:

"Love the Lord your God with all your heart and with all your soul and with all your mind." This is the first and greatest commandment. And the second is like it: "Love your neighbor as yourself." All the Law and the Prophets hang on these two commandments.[14]

That was Jesus's distillation of the entire Old Testament. Add to that the commandment He gave to His disciples before He ascended into heaven. It encapsulates the intent of the New Testament:

All authority in heaven and on earth has been given to me. Therefore go and make disciples of all nations, baptizing them in the name of the Father and of the Son and of the Holy Spirit, and teaching them to obey everything I have commanded you. And surely I am with you always, to the very end of the age.[15]

Using these two touchstones, any Christian can set off in the right direction. Follow this universal purpose, and I believe that in time God will unfold your unique purpose, perhaps as you enter the next level of play.

Major League—Leaning upon God's Favor

The more we depend on God and serve Him, the more we come to understand how God made us and what He is asking us to do. But that isn't what most distinguishes major-league players from minor-league players in the faith journey. What sets them apart is God's favor.

This became clearer to me during a couple of major marking moments with John Maxwell. The first occurred when he let me tag along when he was about to speak to thousands of people. Prior to going out onstage, he went into a room where a group of people he'd never met were waiting for him. They laid hands on him and prayed over him. What struck me in that moment was the humility and dependence John displayed. He was open and receptive, and I didn't sense a bit of self-consciousness.

On our way back to the stage after the prayer, I asked John, "What was that moment about for you?"

"Kevin," John answered, "that's what makes it possible to stand on a stage and see lives changed. God's anointed favor makes all the difference."

That conversation helped me recognize something that resonated in my soul. I saw that a lifetime of chasing God can yield the blessing of God's favor.

The other marking moment with John occurred during a mentoring session. During this particular lunch meeting, my list of questions was long. I was increasingly recognizing the value of leadership, but I was sensing that the value of God's favor was the intangible multiplier on a leader's life. So I asked John, "How do you know God will show up?"

John gave me a blank look. He seemed dumbfounded by my question. "It's never occurred to me that God wouldn't show up."

Now I was the dumbfounded one! As we talked, I realized that the promise that God would be with him was not a cliché to John. It was a way of life, as normal as breathing.

This helped me to gain a better understanding of what it means to remain in the vine. Jesus said, "I am the vine; you are the branches. If you remain in me and I in you, you will bear much fruit; apart from me you can do nothing."[16] If I could chase God as a lifestyle, being dependent on Him and leaning upon His favor, I would never have to wonder if God would be with me. I could rely on the fact that He will never leave or forsake me, something difficult for me to learn as someone with trust issues because of my history with my dad abandoning me in my teen years.

I began to lean into this truth, and it changed the way I lived. The same can be true for you. Once you experience the favor of God, you will never want to go back to Little League faith or minor-league living. You will chase God and lean into His favor because there is nothing else like it. With favor God does for you what you could never do for yourself. It's what set Joseph apart. He couldn't have gone from the pit to the palace without it. It's what made 12Stone's turnaround possible. It's why John Maxwell agreed to mentor someone with a broken background like me. There's nothing like God's favor.

Joshua 23:10 provides my favorite image of God's favor. It says, "One of you routs a thousand, because the LORD your God fights for you." How can a single warrior with one sword take down a thousand armed enemies? Because God fights for him!

I want God fighting for me in my character battles. I want God fighting for my marriage, my kids, my relationships in life. I want God fighting for my career and finances. I want God fighting for me against the rulers, authorities, powers of this dark world, and spiritual forces of evil that Paul writes about in Ephesians 6:12. If the Lord fights these battles using His favor, I have a chance for a home run life. Without God's favor, I'm in trouble.

As we grow and mature in the faith and learn to lean into God's favor, it can become as tangible to us as business success or as the love and joy in marriage. It can bring a practical peace within us that empowers us to withstand any circumstances. We learn that the old church hymn I grew up singing is really true:

O what peace we often forfeit,
O what needless pain we bear,
All because we do not carry,
Everything to God in prayer.[17]

What if we don't learn this lesson? What if we don't move up to a major-league level of dependence on and connection with God? Jesus said, "Apart from me you can do *nothing*."[18] What did He mean by "nothing"? Because obviously we can do something. Many people accomplish much while ignoring God and living far from Him. I believe He meant we can do nothing that *lasts*, nothing that proves to be *fulfilling* or *worthy* of our life investment. If we spend our lives on things that have no eternal value and we exist for our egos, then our efforts will prove to be worth nothing. In the end, everything temporal will burn. Only God can turn our lives into something with true meaning, which means that their impact lasts beyond the mere physical world. He makes it possible via the power of the Holy Spirit for us to be part of His kingdom.

John's Perspective

I don't think that it would be an exaggeration to say that everything good that has happened in my life has been the result of prayer. It began with the covering of my parents. My mother prayed for God's grace and mercy over me from the time I was born. I found early direction in Bible college while preparing for ministry as I spent an hour with God at lunchtime every day. And I cannot adequately express my gratitude for all my prayer partners through the years. While I was at Skyline Church in San Diego, more than one hundred people were praying for me daily, and my friend Bill Klassen interceded for me every day.

John Wesley, possibly the greatest faith leader since the Apostle Paul, said, "God does nothing but in answer to prayer." Throughout my life, each time we moved, I found a new place where I could spend time alone with God, asking His forgiveness, seeking His direction, requesting His blessing and protection on my wonderful family. God has been very kind and given me His favor.

Trust God—Period

If you want to connect with God, you must learn to trust Him. As you trust Him, you will come to learn more of Him. Someone I've seen do that is E.J., my friend Ernie Johnson Jr. He came to 12Stone Church in the late 1990s, and I've watched him progress from unresolved seeker of truth, to new Christian, to amateur-league believer, to minor leaguer, to major leaguer.

Ernie's name may be familiar to you. He is a Turner Sports

broadcaster who has covered Major League Baseball and the NBA, as well as regularly jousting verbally with retired NBA player Charles Barkley. Almost as soon as E.J. came to faith and began learning God's principles and values, he felt a prompt from God to apologize to a television colleague, a producer, whom he had verbally abused early in his career. To his credit, E.J. didn't resist God. As soon as he felt the conviction, he called the producer, told her about his recent conversion, and apologized to her.

Years later as E.J. was moving into the minor league of faith, I watched as he dealt with the sorrow of his son Michael's health decline with muscular dystrophy to the point that Michael became wheelchair-bound. E.J.'s faith and dependence on God just got stronger. Then in the mid-2000s, he got cancer: follicular non-Hodgkins lymphoma. His strong faith and dependence on God deepened. I learned how much one day at the local Starbucks as we talked. "PK," he said—using the shortened version of "Pastor Kevin"—"here's what God is teaching me." He wrote on a napkin as he spoke. "All He wants for me to do is trust Him. Not to trust Him with a blank." He wrote it out: *Trust Him with* _____. "He doesn't want a trust where I fill in the blank and essentially tell Him how to run my life.

"He does not want me to trust Him after He does what I want," E.J. continued. That's the way Jacob first tried to deal with God. "Here's what He wants." He scribbled these words on the napkin: TRUST GOD. He said as he wrote it: "Trust God period."

Wow, I thought. *This is the man who years ago over a grilled chicken salad at O'Charley's said "yes" to Jesus for the first time. And now he's walking through cancer and teaching me.*

E.J.'s faith is major league. To this day, if you get a note from E.J. it's signed, "Trust God, period." And he continues to trust God. In 2010, his wife, Cheryl, felt a prompt to adopt two more children. (They already had four children, two of whom were adopted.) That was another huge commitment—but not too big for people like Ernie and Cheryl who remain dependent on God, are connected to Him, and are always ready and willing to follow His prompts. They are on God's purpose by God's power.

What about you? Have you settled what it means to be "in charge" but not "in control"? Are you "in the vine" and connected to the God who created you? Are you getting on God's purpose by God's power? Are you leaning on His favor? You can. And it will change everything in your life, beginning with helping you win within, which is the subject of the next chapter.

John's Application Guide

Discussion Questions

1. Which of the two brothers, Jacob or Esau, do you most readily identify with? Are you someone who tries to make things happen? Or do you tend to wait for things to happen and then react to them?

2. Why do you think God chose to wrestle with Jacob? Can you think of a time in your life when you felt like you were wrestling with God? Describe it. How long did it last? What was the outcome?

3. What spiritual league do you think you are currently playing in: amateur, minor, or major? Why? What is the key issue you need to deal with to be ready to move up? What are you willing to do to take the next step? How can others help you?

4. Have you ever experienced the favor of God? Explain. What impact did it have on you? How has it changed the way you live day-to-day? If not, what do you think having the favor of God would be like for you personally? What are you prepared to do in order to move up to major-league faith?

(Continued)

5. If you were asked to describe your spiritual batting average, where 1.000 means you feel connected with God 100 percent of the time and .000 means you have never felt connected to God, what number would you say describes you? Explain.
6. Which best describes the way you've been approaching life up to this point:
   A. Trying to accomplish your purpose with your power?
   B. Trying to accomplish your purpose with God's power?
   C. Trying to accomplish God's purpose with your power?
   D. Trying to accomplish God's purpose with His power?

What do you think it will take to get you more on track to trust God, period, and get completely on His agenda?

Assignment
Take your connection with God to new places by doing one of the following.

A. If you haven't already read the Bible in its entirety, begin a reading plan. Choose one of the approaches mentioned in the chapter:
   • Read Genesis, Exodus, Luke, and Acts in the next four months.
   • Read the New Testament in six months.
   • Read the Bible in a year.
B. Kevin did a series at 12Stone Church called "Daniel Days." Using the Old Testament's Daniel as your inspiration, stop to pray three times a day for fifteen minutes. Do this every day for a month. Weave the time with God into your life by seeking Him on a regularly planned schedule. Make sure to journal some of your prayer time so that you have a record of it.

C. Set aside a one-hour block of time every week to wrestle with God. Get away from home or work, be by yourself, and just spend the time interacting with God. When I lived in Ohio, I found a particular rock I liked to sit on while I prayed. Find a place that works for you. Then commit to doing this weekly getaway with God for a specific length of time: a month, six months, a year. Balance your time between Scripture reading and prayer based on which "league" you are currently in. Be sure to record your prayers and observations each time you meet to wrestle with God.

6

First Base: How to Win Within

What happens most of the time at a professional baseball game when a player comes up to bat? The answer is that he fails to reach first base safely. Ted Williams, considered by many to be the greatest hitter of all time, had an extraordinary on-base percentage of .4817. That's a great number in baseball. But it also means that he failed to reach first base more than half of the time he entered the batter's box.

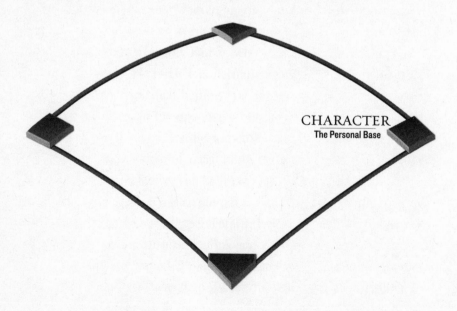

CHARACTER
The Personal Base

When focusing on the spiritual journey, the biggest breakdowns also usually occur on the way to first base. People fail because they don't win character issues. As a result, their relationships break down and their careers flame out. Remember, you can never score in life according to God's game plan unless you can get to first base.

What Blows Up Our Lives?

I watch a lot of movies. I love them for the entertainment factor, but I also often see spiritual truths in them. A favorite lesson can be found in the 2008 movie *Iron Man*. It's the story of Tony Stark, a playboy inventor who inherits his father's fortune and his interest in the weapons manufacturing industry he founded. Though Tony is a genius at creating weapons, he is also a picture of self-indulgence and irresponsibility. To say that he's someone who has neglected first base is an understatement. But his nonchalance toward character does catch up with him, and as is true for all of us, his actions have consequences.

In a pivotal scene of the movie, the military vehicle in which Tony is riding somewhere in Afghanistan is attacked by terrorists, and the convoy is destroyed. Tony runs for his life, only to come face-to-face with a bomb that has been launched by the enemy. To his shock, the bomb has the name and logo of his own company on it. When it explodes, Tony is near-fatally wounded.

What does this have to do with character and first base? The message is painfully clear. We are like Tony Stark: What blows up in our lives usually has our name on it! The problems we experience—we often create. And like Tony, we are often surprised when they blow up in our faces and ruin our lives.

Has that been true for you? Are you surprised by the blowups in your life? Or do you have the eyes to see your own role in creating many of them? Do you have the courage to confess how you contribute to the consequences you experience? If so, you probably understand the connection between consequences and character flaws. Once you understand how you blow up your own dreams, you have good reasons to win first-base character.

Now, I'm not a millionaire playboy, and chances are you're not, either. So if you don't relate to Tony Stark, here's an image that may resonate with you. Character problems are like sinkholes. Sinkholes are fissures or chasms hidden under the surface of the ground that collapse, creating an open hole in the ground. I've read that Florida is full of them. Water erodes the limestone underground and leaves empty pockets. When the ground above them gives way, a hole is created. Some are tiny. But others are big enough to swallow a car, a house, or, according to one article in the *Wall Street Journal*, an entire car dealership! What's amazing is that the moment before the sinkhole opens up, nobody has a clue there is a problem. One minute you're in your house and everything is normal. The next minute, the ground collapses and your house is destroyed.[1]

People who don't take care of character issues are like houses built over sinkholes. They may look great. They may appear solid—not only to the casual observer but also to the residents in the house. But as soon as pressure comes, because the foundation is weak, cracks appear, and total disaster may be only seconds away.

Good character creates an invisible foundation in a person's life, upon which relationships, career, and purpose can be built. With a strong character foundation, you can withstand life's storms and pressures. Without it, you implode and your entire life can get swallowed up like a house in a sinkhole.

John's Perspective

Too many people today worry more about how others see them instead of who they really are. That's a recipe for disaster. My mentor, former UCLA head basketball coach John Wooden, advised, "Be more concerned with your character than your reputation, because your character is what you really are, while your reputation is merely what others think you are."

Always remember that character is a choice. You form it every day by your choices, especially the ones you make when no one is looking. The good choices you make may not be easy, but they always pay off in the long run.

Incredible Promise, Spectacular Implosion

One of the many fantastic things about the Bible is that it not only provides stories of great men and women of the faith who succeeded by the power of God, but also tells unvarnished stories of people who stumbled, fell short, or failed utterly.

One of the most striking examples of character implosion in all of Scripture is Samson from the book of Judges. Even before he was born, Samson was supposed to have a special relationship with God. Judges 13 recounts how an angel of the Lord appeared to Samson's mother, telling her,

> You are barren and childless, but you are going to become pregnant and give birth to a son...The boy is to be a Nazirite, dedicated to God from the womb. He will take the lead in delivering Israel from the hands of the Philistines.[2]

True to God's word, she did conceive and give birth to a son. Scripture says, "He grew and the LORD blessed him, and the Spirit of the LORD began to stir him..."[3]

Unfortunately when Samson grew up, he was strong in body but weak in character. When the Spirit of the Lord was on him, Samson displayed incredible strength. He was able to tear apart a young lion with his bare hands. He was effective in fighting the Philistines. But his character continually undermined him, and even though he was called to lead the people of Israel and deliver them from the Philistines, he kept falling short.

Samson's character failings are stark in the story of his marriage to a Philistine woman. The children of Israel had been commanded in Deuteronomy not to intermarry with the people in the Promised Land after they settled there.[4] Joshua reiterated that admonition, warning the Hebrews, saying:

> But if you turn away and ally yourselves with the survivors of these nations that remain among you and if you intermarry with them and associate with them, then you may be sure that the LORD your God will no longer drive out these nations before you. Instead, they will become snares and traps for you, whips on your backs and thorns in your eyes, until you perish from this good land, which the LORD your God has given you.[5]

This could have been a message written directly to Samson, yet he disregarded it. Samson told his parents, "I have seen a Philistine woman in Timnah; now get her for me as my wife." When they resisted his request, he responded like a spoiled child: "Get her for me. She's the right one for me."[6]

In the end, the Philistine woman Delilah and her countrymen became a trap for Samson. They gouged out his eyes, and no doubt they must have whipped him as they set him to grinding grain in prison.

Set Apart

Where did Samson's problems begin? He crossed lines he shouldn't have, and the more he did so, the more casual he became in violations of character. In a nation that was set apart for God and asked to be holy, Samson was commanded to live by an even higher standard. God drew lines that Samson was never to cross, those of Nazirites, who are told:

> Don't consume anything that comes from a grapevine.
> Don't use a razor on your head.
> Don't go near a dead body.[7]

Samson seemed to think nothing of crossing those lines. He once ate honey from the carcass of a dead lion, a clear violation of God's admonition not to go near a dead body. And then he shared the honey with his parents. When he didn't feel any immediate consequences for his actions, he probably believed none were coming.

That's how the erosion of character works. It is like the erosion of limestone. You may not see it at first. You may not know how bad things are until it's too late and there is a collapse. And even if we *do* get wind of a problem, if we're succeeding in one area of life, we give ourselves permission to neglect another. We get the promotion we want so badly by working eighty hours a week, and excuse ourselves for not worshipping God on the Sabbath, or neglecting our family, or skipping time for prayer and meditation on God's Word. We think, *It's only for a season. I'll make it up later.* But more often than not, a season becomes a lifestyle.

Maybe that's the way Samson thought: *The Nazirite rules are not as important as the main thing.* For him, that main thing was his strength. After all, he was the strongest man in the world at a time when physical strength defined dominance. He killed a thousand men with the jawbone of a donkey![8] He was doing big things. So maybe it didn't seem like a big deal when he ate the honey.

But as soon as we give ourselves permission to cross a line we know we shouldn't, we start to deceive ourselves, and the drip, drip erosion of our character begins. We excuse our choices. Drip. We want others to excuse our choices. *Our circumstances are different*, we think. *God understands.* We lie to ourselves. Drip. And if we lie to ourselves, we will inevitably lie to others. Drip. We become more and more focused on ourselves. We keep distancing ourselves from what's right. Drip. We have to rationalize more and more. Soon we're doing things we *never* thought we'd be okay with. The collapse isn't far behind.

That's where Samson's life went: as he married a woman God had forbidden any Hebrew to wed; as he made a bet with the thirty wedding guests and later struck down thirty men from Ashkelon to pay off the bet; as he took personal revenge on the Philistines; as he committed sexual sins; and as he toyed with his Philistine enemy.

Samson chased what he thought would be the good life and he did it his own way, as we often do. But his life ended up empty. Instead of delivering his nation from the Philistines for good, he ended up sacrificing himself to take out only three thousand of them. How different might it have been if he had surrendered himself to God and allowed God to change him from within?

The Power of a Pencil

It's easy to see that Samson crossed lines he shouldn't have. But what about us? Do we know what lines we should not cross if we want to win within at first base? And who draws those lines? Who defines what is good versus what is evil, right versus wrong, wise versus foolish? I'm not talking about the lines for our nation or for our neighbors. (That's another conversation.) I mean the lines for us personally.

How do you answer those questions? Who draws the lines in your life? Where do you go for answers to character questions? Do you look to...

A. The media and political polls
B. Your friends' collective wisdom
C. Your family
D. Your feelings
E. A political party
F. Educators and schools
G. Religious leaders
H. God's Word
I. Whatever seems good in your own eyes
J. Other

This is an important question, because whoever controls the "pencil" in your life draws the lines. If you haven't given God that power in your life, then you don't know where His lines are and you don't live by them. If that's the case, you will get called out before you ever reach first base.

I think many of us would like to think that lines don't matter. For many of us, if we come across a line we don't like, we ignore it. Or we try to erase it and redraw our own. Why would we think that can work at first base? It doesn't work anywhere else in life. God created the entire game of life, and everywhere you look there are lines. Some are hardwired into the universe: the speed of light, the laws of physics, mathematical properties. But there are lines drawn in every area of society, too: companies, banks, cultures, sports. The game of baseball is full of lines: foul lines, base lines, batter's box lines, home run fence lines. And the game is won and lost within those lines. Of course God has drawn lines. And we violate them at our peril.

As each of my first three kids approached sixteen years of age, they were so eager to get their license to drive. I was a concerned (and sometimes terrified) parent, so I had the learn-to-drive conversation with them. I knew they were thinking of their new freedoms, while I was thinking of their new responsibilities. As each child approached driver's training, I explained to them that freedom comes with lines. It went something like this:

A car is life and death. When you get your license, you are going to feel a freedom unlike anything you have known. It is awesome and I am happy for you. The freedom of driving feels like being let out of prison. A driver's license is life giving. Equally, the car is like a weapon. When you don't know how to handle it, when you're foolish with it, when you misjudge it, when you drive outside the lines, it can cause death. I've lost friends to accidents. I lost my brother. So the freedom of driving comes with a universal agreement that there are lines on the road that cannot be crossed. When you cross those lines, everyone loses.

My sister was sixteen when a drunk driver came over a hill at sixty miles an hour, crossing over the yellow line. He hit my sister's car head-on. The resulting wreck landed my sister and her friend in the hospital. The drunk driver lost his life. When I saw the condition of the cars after the accident, I thought, *Nobody should've lived through that one.* All that loss and death because someone crossed a line that should never have been crossed.

I love my kids, so I helped them understand the lines on the road. God our Father loves us, and for that reason, He shows us where the lines are and asks us not to cross them. That is part of His game plan for life to the full. When we stay within them, we can keep the ball in play and win. We can have a home run life. When God drew the lines for Samson and Israel, He was trying to give them life. If they had paid attention and fought to honor the lines God gave them, they would have had the entire Promised Land. If we pay attention to God's lines and fight to keep from crossing them, it will help us build our career, marriage, family, health, and spiritual well-being. We need to acknowledge God as the one who holds the pencil.

Lifelines

The lines God draws are lifelines. They help us to live well and win character issues, which sets us up for the rest of life. When the New Testament church was born, as described in the book of Acts, there were many conversations about moral lines. All of those help us. But we are fortunate to also have the help of the Holy Spirit. With the help of these two lifelines—the Bible and the Holy Spirit—I believe we can discern two types of lines that will help us to win within and get on first base.

1. Solid Lines—Wrong for Everyone

God has drawn many solid lines for us. The purpose of this kind of line is to communicate that crossing it is a sin for everyone. This is like the double yellow line on a highway. Crossing it brings death.

When we read 1 Corinthians 5, we see that the Apostle Paul points out an indisputable solid line to the church. He addresses sexual immorality being practiced by someone in the church who calls himself a believer. Paul wants to make it clear that sexual immorality is a line of sin no believer should cross. He tells the Corinthians to get rid of sin, and if this person who says he's a believer will not agree to honor this line from God, then he must be expelled from that circle of faith.

But isn't that judging? you may ask. I believe Paul addresses this. Once we come under Christ, we agree with God's lines. While nobody walks this perfectly, it is our objective in life to walk in God's ways. In this way, we're like baseball players. We try to play without making errors, yet from time to time we may drop the ball. An error is never the goal. Nor would we ever call an error a good play. And just as a baseball player's labeling an error as good would be wrong, so would it be wrong for a Christ follower to call something good that God calls sin. Knowing good from bad is discerning God's truth, not judging. Believers not acknowledging the difference create problems in the faith community.

The focus on lines from Paul in this passage is entirely on followers of Christ. In fact, Paul clarifies that he is not encouraging a judgmental spirit toward the unbelieving world. He expects them to go their own way. He writes, "What business is it of mine to judge those outside the church?" The implied answer is none. Paul writes, "God will judge those outside." People inside the church are a different matter. Paul continues, "Expel the wicked person from among you."[9] In other words, if someone in the church ignores God's solid lines or tries to erase them, they don't belong with other believers.

When Scripture is clear about sin, we must acknowledge that God has drawn a solid line. Paul was clear on this. Pay attention to the language Paul uses in Colossians 3:5–10:

Put to death, therefore, whatever belongs to your earthly nature: sexual immorality, impurity, lust, evil desires and greed, which is idolatry. Because of these, the wrath of God is coming. You used to walk in these ways, in the life you once lived. But now you must also rid yourselves of all such things as these: anger, rage, malice, slander, and filthy language from your lips. Do not lie to each other, since you have taken off your old self with its practices and have put on the new self, which is being renewed in knowledge in the image of its Creator.

The lesson is clear: Don't try to erase or redefine what God has made a solid line. That's what cost Samson. He ignored God's lines so he could indulge his desires. He talked like a follower of God but lived like a Philistine. If we do that we will blow up our lives, just as Samson did.

2. Dotted Lines—Wrong for Me

Solids lines are very clear, and if we want to follow God, our only choice is to respect them. But not all the lines God draws are solid. Some are dotted. What does that mean? It means that some things are a sin for some people but not for everyone.

We can see this in Samson's life. During his time, the Ten Commandments served as God's solid lines for everyone in Israel. However, God drew a dotted line for Samson. He was supposed to abstain from any drink that came from grapes. That was a sin for him. Was it a sin for everyone else? No. Cutting his hair was a sin. Was it for everyone else? No. To truly follow God, Samson needed to obey the solid lines as well as the dotted lines God had just for him.

God continues to draw dotted lines for us. For you something may be a sin. For me it may not be. And vice versa. For example, part of my vow as a pastor in my circle includes a commitment to abstain from alcohol. More important, that was also something I sensed the Lord asking of me in my college years. So I knew for me to consume alcohol would be a sin. However, let's be clear: Nowhere in the Bible does it teach that a beverage with alcohol is sinful to drink. What does it say? Paul writes in 1 Corinthians,

> Or do you not know that wrongdoers will not inherit the kingdom of God? Do not be deceived: Neither the sexually immoral nor idolaters nor adulterers, nor men who have sex with men nor thieves nor the greedy nor *drunkards* nor slanderers nor swindlers will inherit the kingdom of God. And that is what some of you were. But you were washed, you were sanctified, you were justified in the name of the Lord Jesus Christ and by the Spirit of our God. [emphasis added][10]

So getting drunk is a sin. It's a solid line for everyone without exception. But having a drink with alcohol is a dotted line biblically. So you must settle with God's leading what is pleasing and profitable in your walk with Him.

We should never call something a dotted line that God has labeled a solid line. Neither should we call something a solid line when God has labeled it a dotted line. I do not have the freedom to tell others that drinking a beer is a sin just because God made it clear to me that I am not to do it. Many of my friends enjoy a cold beer or a glass of wine over dinner. I'm not in the least offended by that. Nor do I prefer they not drink around me. I don't even think that abstaining from alcohol is a sign of greater holiness. It's simply a decision God asked of me. So, believe it or not, I have never had a drink of alcohol in my life.

If you want to win your character battles within, you need to worry about observing the dotted lines God has given you without trying to impose them on everyone else.

Getting Practical at First Base

Working within the lines God provides is the overarching guideline for living as a follower of Christ and is the start of winning within at first base. But what do you do day-to-day to win character battles? I suggest that you consistently engage in four practices:

1. *Pay*, Then Play

We live in a world where people are encouraged to play now and worry little about what may happen tomorrow. That's what Samson did. He indulged himself first, never really expecting his actions to catch up with him. But they did. They *always* do. The first rule of character is learning how to become self-led. If you do not learn to lead yourself, you will be a slave to other people and things. And you will never learn to lead others in marriage, family, work, faith, or life.

There's an insightful line in the movie *The Great Debaters*: "We do the things we don't want to do, so we can do the things we want to do." In other words, they choose to pay first so that they can play later. If you do your homework before you go out to play, then you fully enjoy your play. And you benefit from always having your school-work done on time. If you get your work done for your job before you take your vacation, you serve your company well, advancing its cause. And you can truly relax as you enjoy your time off. In your finances, if you live by the 10–10–80 principle—where you give your first 10 percent to God through your church, put 10 percent away as savings, and then live on the remaining 80 percent—then you enjoy financial stability and open up your life to God's blessing. Paying first *always* benefits you.

In contrast, if you always play first, then your life becomes chaotic and guilt-ridden. If you play first, there will be times when you don't get your homework done. To compensate, you either cheat another part of your life or do poorly in school, which usually sets off a chain reaction of negative consequences.

If you put vacation and recreation ahead of your work, you cheat your employer, let down your co-workers and customers, and undermine your career. If it costs you your job, you lose not only the resources to play in the future, but also the means to support yourself.

If you spend your income on indulgences and live beyond your means, you fall short in paying your bills, you put yourself in debt, and you have no financial margin for life's everyday difficulties and setbacks. You never actually make money, because you do that only when you save. You also have nothing left to give God, which Scripture says is robbing Him![11] That makes it nearly impossible for Him to freely bless you!

In my first few years in ministry, I came across a statement about discipline that changed how I viewed life. It was attributed to Jim Rohn: "There are two types of pain in this world, the short term pain of discipline and the long term pain of regret. One weighs ounces, the other tons. Choose your pain."

Don't try to kid yourself. You must choose because no one escapes both. Everyone pays. Either you pay on the front end, when the price is lower and you have more choices in how you pay, or you pay on the back end, when the price is higher and the choices are few.

Samson could have ruled Israel with power and been a blessing to his people. He could have gone about doing that in any number of ways—if he had been willing to pay the price. All he had to do was live within the lines God had drawn for him. Instead, he played. It cost him his strength, his freedom, his sight, and in the end his life. Yet all along, God had a better life in mind for Samson. God had more, but Samson never got it. What is the *more* that God might have for you, if only you will discipline yourself to pay first?

John's Perspective

When I was growing up, my father often told us, "Pay now, play later." That was not an easy lesson for me to learn. I was a very sanguine kid and I loved to play. I could have spent every day of my childhood shooting hoops and playing with my friends. In fact, I think I did.

The lesson of paying first did not really sink in for me until one particular Saturday morning. It was my job as a child to clean the basement. I had to do that every week. My dad, in an effort to train us in self-reliance, allowed us to decide when we would do our chores. So I could clean the basement any day of the week. But the rule was that I had to be finished by noon Saturday.

One particular week, I put off cleaning the basement every day. *I'll do it tomorrow*, I said to myself each day as I went out to play.

The deadline came, as it always does, and I had not done my work. At noon my dad loaded up the car with my mom, my brother, and my sister—everyone in the family except me—to spend the afternoon swimming. I'll never forget watching them drive off together.

I never put off doing my chores again.

2. Win Three-Second Windows

I grew up in a home where my father had a volcanic temper. When he was fed up, he'd blow up. My brothers and I followed suit. We would blow up when it suited us, and we justified our anger. We would blame circumstances, other people, or problems, saying they *caused* us to lose our temper. "You make me mad!" I would say, as if someone else was responsible for my rage. But losing your temper is a choice. People can do things that light a fire, but you have to agree to be the fuel that makes them blow up. It's a choice.

When I went to Bible college, I carried my temper with me. I once lost a simple game in the recreation room, which made me mad. So I put my fist through a wall. Literally! Months later, I was called into the college president's office because of my actions. The president told me how disappointed he was in me. What was my response? I proceeded to let him know how disappointed I was in him. To this day, I am embarrassed by the disrespect I showed the president. But when you lack self-control, then you'll say and do stupid things.

By the time Marcia and I said "I do," I had forged my temper into a tool to try to force her into my way of thinking. What I didn't know was that I married an unintimidated lady who had no intention of conforming to my expectations. You can imagine how well that went. I'll explain more in the next chapter as we look at the people base.

Why do I mention these conflicts and character missteps? Because they were preventable. I had a choice not to allow my temper to run wild, undermine my character, and damage my relationships. All I had to do was make the right choice in a two- to three-second window.

What do I mean by a three-second window? In the midst of every temptation, there is a moment when your emotions are at their peak and giving in to temptation seems like the right thing to do. If you know that this onslaught of seemingly unendurable temptation is coming and you train yourself to wait it out, though, you can overcome it.

For me, in those seconds I told myself that if I just blew up then I'd feel better and it would "solve" my problem. That was a lie. When I learned to anticipate that lie, to expect it, to endure the two or three seconds of intensity it brought, and wait it out, then my temper would begin to subside. And I would avoid doing the things that were harming my character and relationships. The key is to expect it and know it will pass, because whenever temptation comes and you give in, it builds upon itself and becomes even worse. It's like unleashing a monster.

A simple illustration with a balloon may help you understand how this works. Temptation builds like a balloon filling with air. When we feel that the balloon can't take any more, we want to let it loose so that it deflates. But what happens when you let go of a full balloon? It flies around, zipping back and forth, up and down, and bangs against everything in its path until the air is gone and the balloon drops to the floor! When I lost my temper, I acted like the balloon—or the buffoon, if you prefer. In those moments, I often said to myself, *This is impossible to control.* And that was true—after I'd let my temper go. Try it. Fill a balloon, let it go, and *then* try to control it. It is impossible. The time to control it is *before* letting it go. If you can hold on to the balloon and let the air out slowly, you solve the problem. You do that by winning that three-second window before you let the balloon go.

This makes all the difference in the world. God made it clear that I had to win this small window of time to control my temper. Yes, I grew up in a volatile home. While that may *explain* my temper, it does not *excuse* my temper. And that was a life-changing confession. I recognized that God had drawn a line. I was to put away rage, malice, and anger.[12] I had to practice self-control in this area to win first base.

To help me win this, I memorized two Scriptures and repeated them to myself during the three-second windows when I was tempted to blow up. The first was 1 Corinthians 10:13: "No temptation has overtaken you except what is common to mankind. And God is faithful; he will not let you be tempted beyond what you can bear. But when you are tempted, he will also provide a way out so that you can endure it." I trained myself to embrace the truth that any temptation I experienced from the evil one could not be greater than the power of God within me. I just needed to depend on Him—the lesson of home plate. So when the tension rose, I claimed this verse as my promise. And I bolstered it with the second verse I memorized, which was Proverbs 15:1: "A gentle answer turns away wrath, but a harsh word stirs up anger." I admit that this may seem very simple, but it started to change me. Where my temper had continually caused me to strike out in the area of character, I was finally winning within and reaching first base.

The idea of winning a three-second window applied to nearly every temptation I was facing. It worked with lust, impulse buying, impulse eating, and other temptations. And I believe it will work to help you win at first base. What is your primary area of temptation? What might change in your life if you were able to consistently win over it? Try winning the three-second window.

3. Have No Secret World

One of the most destructive things any person can do is create a secret life where they cross God's lines. Secret sin in my dad's life is one of the main things that caused the blowup of my parents' marriage. Our family appeared one way at church on Sunday and a completely different way every other day of the week. It was a sham.

Secret sins always hurt you and others. They create sinkholes that quietly undermine your character until there is a collapse that destroys you and threatens to suck in the other people around you.

That was what happened to Tiger Woods several years ago. He created a secret life, and when it was exposed, his life collapsed. We talked a lot about Tiger in my home because my son Jake loves golf and greatly admired Tiger's ability when he was at his peak. Jake would record Tiger's matches and watch them with devotion. Tiger was a modern-day Samson—*the* dominant golfer in the world at one time. Nobody else even came close. He won all four majors in a twelve-month span of time. Thousands, if not millions, of people would have gladly traded places with him. He was the best in the world at his profession and worth half a billion dollars. He had achieved a gentleman's reputation that made him a gold mine for the game of golf and its advertisers.

What most people never suspected was that he was descending into deception. He wanted it all: career, wealth, marriage, and family. But he also wanted the indulgence of Delilah. Though he was winning huge at third base, he was compromising at first base. And of course, it blew up his life. He put his career on hold to try to save his marriage and family. But this didn't work, and like Samson he lost his strength. Who knows how long it will take for Woods's "hair" to grow back and for him to dominate again?

Jake still plays on his high school golf team, and he still records and watches Tiger. While both Jake and I would like to see Tiger do well, our conversations helped my teenage son realize nobody can have a home run life if he cheats at first base. No one is exempt, not even the Samson of golf. And that's not a judgment, that's a humbling reality for us all. If we maintain a secret life, we will crash at first base.

Long ago I discovered a significant truth in life: I am only as sick as my secrets. Any sin that you keep secret will slowly but steadily erode your character. Secret sin creates sinkholes in a person's life. I have seen too many people create private worlds for themselves, especially people who have freedom or money. For that reason, I do not allow myself to create secrets in any area of life. I open my life to accountability and input from more mature believers. I don't keep secrets from my wife. I am open about my temptations to my prayer partner, Dave Bearchell, and to others I respect.

You need to do the same. You need to open up your life to mature believers who can help you. That takes humility, openness, courage, and trust. It's difficult to open yourself up for correction in areas where you know you need to change. But it's one of the most important ways you can guard and build your character so that you can win at first base.

John's Perspective

The year 1987 stands out for me because several high-profile church leaders fell morally. At that time, I was the senior pastor of Skyline Church. It was heartbreaking to see these things happen. I

(Continued)

remember thinking, *That could never happen to me.* Then I read that one of the men who fell said, "I thought that this could never happen to me." That was a sobering moment.

To guard against moral failure, I put five practices into place:

1. I seldom travel alone.
2. I call my wife, Margaret, every night.
3. I am seldom alone with a woman.
4. I talk positively about Margaret.
5. I choose my close friends carefully.

I also vowed to never have any kind of secret life. I have no secrets from Margaret, and I try to live my life as an open book.

4. Put Purity Over Passion

God calls His people to be holy because He is holy. He wants us to be like Him. But He is also teaching us lessons on faithfulness. God asks us to be spiritually faithful, with only one God. If we are faithful to Him, we don't hurt ourselves unnecessarily. Likewise, if we are sexually faithful, with only one spouse, we cause less harm to ourselves and others. Sexual promiscuity can lead to betrayal, heartache, pain, and disease. It can and does destroy families and create societal chaos.

The desire to go outside the lines that God gives us is as old as the human race. The simple fact that the Old Testament tells people not to engage in adultery, homosexuality, incest, and other forms of sexual sin is proof that people have wanted to engage in those practices for thousands of years, just as they do now. Human nature hasn't changed. Neither have the lines God has drawn for us. Purity has been and always will be God's standard. That's why we need to fight for it.

One of the best moments in John's ministry occurred when he sat down on the stage at a Promise Keepers event and had a candid conversation about purity. I've asked him to share it here.

John's Perspective

In 1994, I was asked to speak for Promise Keepers at an event at the Hoosier Dome in Indianapolis. The subject selected for me was moral purity.

From the time that I accepted the assignment and began writing my message, I felt sexual temptation unlike anything I had ever encountered before. I felt like the enemy was trying to take me out or discredit me before the event.

In his book *Temptation*, Dietrich Bonhoeffer says, "When lust takes control, at that moment God is quite unreal to us." I did everything I could to guard against lust. I spent extra time with God. And I also did something I had never done before. I asked my children, who were teenagers at the time, to pray for me in the area of temptation. "I have always been faithful to your mother," I told them, "and I always will be with God's help." Each night as they got ready to go to bed, we prayed together, and their prayers strengthened me.

When the day of the event finally arrived, I was excited. God had taken care of me. I had made it through the storm, and I was ready. So was the audience of fifty-five thousand people. They were fired up. I'll never forget that day. The title of my talk was "Leave Your Jacket," and it centered on the story of Joseph and Potiphar's wife. The first point in my section on how to handle sexual temptation was a single word: Run! When I said it, the crowd went crazy. They cheered continuously for what felt like five minutes.

The truth is that sin will take you farther than you want to go. It will keep you longer than you want to stay. And it will cost you more than you want to pay. And if those thoughts aren't sobering enough to you, then think of your children, if you have any. Whatever you do *will* impact their lives. The legacy they receive from you is determined by your actions today. Will that legacy be positive or negative? The choice is yours.

As followers of Christ, it is our responsibility to know where God has drawn the lines and live in such a way that we do not cross them. What's the best way to do that? We need to identify where the lines are in the cold light of day and commit to staying on the right side of the line before temptation comes. I've always told my children, "Draw the boundary line while you are in your right mind rather than when you are in the heat of the moment. Because if you haven't settled that before the passion hits, you won't know where the line is until you've already crossed it. And then you're in trouble. Once you've crossed a line, you can't *uncross* it!"

If You Can, Win It Early

One of the people I've watched navigate the challenging years of young adulthood is Brandon McCormick. He is a fantastic example of someone who has started well in how he runs the bases beginning in his teen years. He grew up at 12Stone Church from the time his family moved to Georgia when he was ten. Brandon was a kid who was easily distracted and hated school. But when he was fifteen, he found his calling in life: making movies. From that time on, he put his all into learning about filmmaking and creating videos and films.

By the time Brandon was in his late teens, Hollywood was already calling. At that age, many of his filmmaking peers did what most people in our culture do: run straight to third base, cheating the other bases while chasing success. Brandon went in a different direction. He decided to stay in Georgia and pursue a home run life, not merely a season of success. He made a decision to put God first and give God the pencil to draw his lifelines.

Brandon served our church by providing videos before YouTube. When he was good enough to carry storytelling on-screen, the church hired him full-time. He was only eighteen years old. At twenty, he married his high school sweetheart, Kimmie, and they settled down just a few miles away from both of their families. A few years later, he started Whitestone Motion Pictures where he creates innovative content on a shoestring, further honing his craft. All the while, he has stayed connected to God, the church, and spiritual mentors.

Brandon is the ripe old age of...twenty-eight, and already has more than a decade of experience making films. He has developed a team of filmmakers at Whitestone Motion Pictures, and enjoys family life with his wife and two young daughters. His film work has won some thirty awards in the industry, attracting the attention of producers and investors. (If you're curious, you can check out his short films and projects at whitestonemp.com.)

What God will do in and through Brandon's life is not certain. His story is still being written. But what sets him apart from many of his peers is that he is choosing to fight for first-base wins in his life. He didn't take shortcuts. He didn't sell his soul to build a quick career. Instead, he fought the difficult battle of building a character foundation. Brandon wants someday to build a George Lucas–type empire in the foothills of the Appalachians. I don't know if he'll be able to get there. It's too soon to tell. I can already see that he is living life to the full. He's running life's bases the right way—God first, character next, family after that, and career in its rightful place.

Overcoming Your Errors

How are you doing in this area? Are you depending on God and fighting for character wins first? Are you trying to honor God's lines? If you're young, like Brandon, and you fight to win within at first base, you set yourself up for success in every area of life.

But what if you're already older than Brandon? What if you've already made many mistakes? Everyone has wins in some areas and errors in others. Marcia and I won in the area of purity. We married as virgins. But we made a lot of mistakes in other areas. Nobody plays the game of life error-free.

I received a lesson on this in sixth grade when I played for our community baseball team. I played catcher. I'll never forget: There were two outs and the other team had a man on first. The batter had two strikes. One more, and we would finish the inning.

The batter swung and missed on his third strike. But somehow the ball disappeared: It wasn't in my glove or anywhere on the ground. Seeing that I had not caught the ball, the batter ran to first and the other runner advanced all the way to third. Meanwhile, I was looking everywhere for a ball that could not be found. The runner scored, and finally the baseball was discovered. It had gone into my chest protector and lodged there. I was charged with an error. Funny, but not fun!

Years later when I was in my twenties, I played center field for our church softball team. During a game, a batter hit a ball sky-high to deep center. No problem: I was under it. The ball landed in my glove— and popped out. I was so shocked by the error that I froze. The runners advanced.

I was a bit numb as the next batter came up. Sure enough, he hit the ball to deep center. This time I was ready. I got under the ball, it went straight into my glove—and it popped out. I was horrified. I was in shock. This had never happened to me in my life. I started shaking. I knew it was only recreational softball, but I had an ego. I'm competitive and I like winning!

The next batter? Yep, center field. I held on to that ball like it was a multimillion-dollar lottery ticket. I was charged with two errors while the opposing team added two runs. The good news? I got redemption in the next inning when I hit a home run that drove in several runs and helped me get over my errors.

Where am I going with this? I was given a second chance in that game, and I needed it. And though we do not deserve it, God gives second chances. I believe the Apostle John was helping us learn how to make first base our goal, but if and when we stumble, drop the ball, commit an error, or get thrown out on the way to first base, God gives a second chance. He will forgive our sin if we humbly confess. John wrote,

> My dear children, I write this to you so that you will not sin. But if anybody does sin, we have an advocate with the Father— Jesus Christ, the Righteous One. He is the atoning sacrifice for our sins, and not only for ours but also for the sins of the whole world.[13]

And let's not forget: John was writing this to believers, not unbelievers. God anticipates that we will make errors. His desire is for us to turn to Him when we do.

That was the case for Michael. I met him one weekend when my family was out of town. I wanted to get away and finish writing my weekend teaching, so I jumped on my Harley-Davidson motorcycle and rode for an hour. I stopped at a town thirty minutes from 12Stone. I'd never visited this restaurant before, but the waiter was attentive and the food was good. Halfway through my meal, the waiter asked, "Are you the pastor at 12Stone?" When I said yes, he responded, "Man I wanted to thank you guys at 12Stone. A couple of years back, I was doing well in my career. I was manager of a local restaurant and rising. But in private I was crossing a line. Illegal drugs. It was supposed to be fun and I turned out to be the fool. I blew up my life and landed in jail.

"While I was in jail," he continued, "a guy named Russell from 12Stone came every week and brought your teaching DVD. He opened our lives to faith in Jesus. God is changing my life, and since I got out, I've been trying to come to church as much as possible. I'm in a recovery group and I've been clean for months. I just wanted to say thanks for all that you at 12Stone are doing to give people a second chance."

Now, that was even better than a ride on my Harley—and that's saying a lot! But that's God's good news. When our lives blow up— even by our own hand, even when we are already on God's team and commit errors—God will give us a second chance if we are truly repentant. And the truth is, even as believers, we need many second chances. But if we're willing to do things God's way, we will eventually get on first base. We can become a person who lives by the truth and wins the battles within. And when we do, we're in position to win with others on second base, which is the subject of the next chapter, so keep reading.

John's Application Guide

Discussion Questions

1. Have you ever known someone whose life collapsed? If so, what character issues might have undermined that person similar to the sinkhole illustration in the chapter?

2. When you read about Samson's life, do you identify with him? Or do you have a hard time understanding why someone who was selected by God for a special purpose would throw it away the way he did? Explain.

3. Everyone's view of right and wrong has been influenced by factors other than God's Word. Which influences listed in the chapter have had the greatest influence on you? Here is the list from the chapter to jog your memory:

   A. The media and political polls
   B. Your friends' collective wisdom
   C. Your family
   D. Your feelings
   E. A political party
   F. Educators and schools
   G. Religious leaders

    H. God's Word

    I. Whatever seems good in your own eyes

    J. Other

      Have some of these influences gotten you off track in any area of your life? If so, explain.

4. Where has God drawn a dotted line in your life? How did you come to recognize it? How well have you honored it? How has that impacted your life?

5. Which of the four practices recommended in the chapter do you find easiest to do? Which do you find to be most difficult? Why?
   - Pay, Then Play
   - Win Three-Second Windows
   - Have No Secret World
   - Put Purity Ahead of Passion

6. Which of the four practices are you willing to fight for now? How will you go about doing it? Who will you invite to help you engage in the process?

Assignment

Nobody can win character issues alone. All people need the help of mature believers who are ahead of them. Unfortunately, the greater the difficulty you've had winning within at first base, the less inclined you may be to let others into your life to help you.

    If you are not part of a local church, your first assignment is to find one and get connected. And by the way, don't look for a perfect church, because, as Kevin says to people who visit 12Stone, "If you are looking for the perfect church, you did not find it. And you might as well quit looking, because if you find it and join it, you'll ruin it!"

(Continued)

When looking for a church, the most important things are to find one that bases its teachings solidly on the Bible and whose mission, values, and leadership you buy into. Once you find one, then stick with it. For most people who hop from church to church, the issue is them, not the church.

Once you engage with a church, become an active participant. Join a small group. Serve. Support the church financially. Then expect problems and conflict. In the midst of trials is where God will grow you.

If you are already part of a local church, then intentionally seek out mature believers to help you grow in character. Allow them to get to know you. Invite them to point out your character issues. Then commit yourself to doing whatever it takes to obey God and change.

These steps will likely be some of the most significant in your spiritual journey. They will help you to mature in your faith and develop the full life that Jesus promised.

Second Base: How to Win with Others

What are some of your favorite moments in life? The ones that brought great joy? The ones with great meaning? The ones that are most memorable or fun? Do you have three or four of them in mind? Okay, now answer this: How many involve people?

COMMUNITY
The People Base

It Was the Best of Times, It Was the Worst of Times

I don't know about you, but all of mine have people at the center of them. Moments like the first building for 12Stone. After years of struggling in multiple rented facilities, in our seventh year we moved into a ten-thousand-square-foot building with 175 people. On that opening day we filled the 250-seat room to overflowing. We pulled out every chair we owned and set chairs in the lobby. We served 501 people, including adults, students, and children. We finally broke through! Everyone had worked so hard to make that possible. There was such a celebration of gratitude toward God and for our great volunteers. I'll never forget it!

I also think of my wedding day. We thought we looked so good on that day, but now the photographs are a source of humor for our kids. Marcia had her '80s hairstyle; I had my Afro.

And the birth of each child is a treasured memory. So are family vacations when everything went right—as well as when everything went wrong. Like the day we went to the Painted Desert in Arizona with some friends and planned an elaborate picnic. It was part of a seventeen-day pop-up camper road trip to the Grand Canyon and back. We went way over budget to get really good food for the picnic. We picked out the most expensive steaks the store had and packed them in our high-tech cooler that could cool or heat. All you had to do was match blue with blue to cool or red with red to heat.

When we arrived at the picnic site hours later and pulled the cooler out of our friends' SUV, do you know what we found? You guessed it. My friend had reversed the colors and had heated the contents instead of cooling them. The entire lunch was nasty, the meat was disgusting, and we threw it all out. It was the worst picnic ever—but one of our best memories and a favorite story to tell years later.

Every one of my best life experiences involved other people. Now answer this: What are the two or three things from your life that give you the most pain? The experiences that carry disappointment or sorrow? If you're like me, again these involve people. And sometimes the very relationships that provide joy also provide heartache. From harsh words to hurt feelings, from betrayal to divorce, from estrangement to death, relationships can bring as much sorrow as they do happiness.

I don't think it's an overstatement to say that life's highest highs and lowest lows involve other people. And much of that joy or sorrow is created by us in how we develop relationships.

If we could win relationships and live in community with love, peace, and harmony, life would be fantastic! In church circles, it's often said that ministry would be easy if it weren't for the people. But then that seems true everywhere in life:

Leadership would be easy if it weren't for other people.
Work would be easy if it weren't for other people.
Family would be easy if it weren't for other people.
Life would be easy if it weren't for other people.

So why are relationships so hard? Because most of us are broken. We are imperfect people. Everybody has hurts, wounds, and pain that they have to deal with in life, and we bring all that into our relationships. That makes relationships difficult.

John's Perspective

The greatest challenges and the greatest rewards in my life and my leadership have come from people. As a leader, I recognize that any organization's most appreciable asset is people. But that's only if they are appreciated—and developed. Sometimes that means helping them acquire new skills. Other times it means helping them overcome emotional or relational obstacles. That can be difficult, but few things in life are more rewarding than helping others reach their potential.

Hurting People

When I entered into my full-time career in ministry in the mid-1980s, the ideals of leading a church gave way to the realities. One of the more defining discoveries was that hurting people hurt people—and are easily hurt. People in pain lash out. While this sentiment seems to have become more common in recent years, it was a fresh and new idea twenty-five years ago. And my discovery of it changed my perspective on life and relationships.

I mentioned in chapter 2 that my family came apart through my parents' divorce. This was something that had been brewing for a long time, going all the way back to when my parents were in high school and my mother got pregnant. Both my parents quit school without graduating. By the time Mom was twenty-one, she had three boys under age three. I was the third.

Their lack of wisdom and preparation combined with their own baggage kept piling up. Even though Dad came to Christ, he never came clean on his secret sins. It was like the drip, drip creation of a sinkhole. Eventually it eroded the relationship enough to create a cave-in.

The divorce become final when I was twelve, and the family went separate ways. My two older brothers went with Dad. That marked me, but what I did not know at the time was that it wounded me. I had to become a dad myself before I understood the indictment that someone once made of me: "You have daddy issues."

I didn't know it then, but now I recognize that when a boy is in the developing stages of manhood, and the father who is supposed to pour into him doesn't, it leaves the boy emotionally starving and emaciated. As a result, the boy will fail to develop healthy relational "muscles," and he'll be less capable of carrying meaningful relationships than someone with a healthy background.

When I was in my teens and twenties, I didn't know how to win honest, healthy relationships. And as a hurting person, I tended to hurt other people because I was easily angered, felt insecure, and always had something to prove. Further, I tended to be easily hurt by others. In my late twenties, even when inconsequential things happened, I often found myself saying, "That person hurt me!"

I finally started to realize that other people weren't the problem. I was. To help me understand this, God gave me a picture. He brought to my memory a time in sixth grade when I got a sliver (or splinter) in my pinkie. I hid it from my parents because my dad would've just taken a knife and dug it out! I hated pain. So I left it in there and hoped it would get better. But you can guess what happened. It turned red, festered, and got swollen as infection set in.

When one of my brothers barely brushed against it—an action that might not even be noticed by a healthy person—I shouted, "Ow! You hurt me!"

When Mom heard that, she wanted to know what had happened, and then the whole thing went bad. Dad became a surgeon at the kitchen table and dug it out. Only this time, everything was so sensitive that even touching it left me in tears. It was a day I hated and will never forget. Did my brother who barely brushed my injured finger really do wrong? No. But the pain I experienced was real just the same.

This is similar to what often goes on in our relationships. From marriage to family to work to church, many people have neglected and untreated emotional wounds that cause them to be overly sensitive in a certain area of their life. And that's what happened with me. As an adult, I carried around the wound of my parents' divorce like the sliver in my finger. As a result, my interactions with other people were often strained and dysfunctional.

Once you understand this dynamic, you can figure out why emotionally injured people overreact—and it may have nothing to do with their actual situation. They lash out or withdraw because of the pain they feel. And don't be fooled: Time does not heal all wounds. When emotional pain is left untreated, the wound often gets deeper. Emotionally speaking, it descends into dysfunction. So winning at second base begins with the admission that we are imperfect people who have some kind of emotional wounds that need to be healed. But we also need to see healthy relationships modeled and emulate them.

John helped me a great deal with this. He has modeled healthy relationships. He has mentored me through some of my dysfunction. And he has written books that have helped me greatly in this area, including *Relationships 101*, *The 5 Levels of Leadership*, and *The 17 Indisputable Laws of Teamwork*. Two other books that I have found invaluable are *Safe People* and *Boundaries,* both by Henry Cloud and John Townsend. It's taken a lot of hard work, but with God's help I've healed from the wounds that damaged me emotionally, and as a result the relationships in every area of my life have improved. If you have wounds, you may need to do the same.

Dysfunctional to the Core

Think of the most dysfunctional family you've ever met. No matter how bad they are, I bet they don't compare with the most dysfunctional family recorded in Scripture: the family of Jacob.

We tend to talk about biblical figures with a kind of impressed awe, focusing on the highlights of their lives. It's true that Jacob prayed and God showed up in person. The man wrestled with God. He was blessed, and God changed his name, calling him Israel from then on because he was a changed man. His children were the fathers of the twelve tribes of Israel. His is a rags-to-riches story; he went from impoverished exile to incredible wealth with God's favor on him. Wow! What a résumé.

But there's also another side to his story that's not always pretty.

And it has lessons to teach us about relationships. Jacob's first recorded "success" was the manipulation of his brother, Esau, so that he could take his birthright.[1] Later Jacob lied to his father and deceived him—with the help of his mother—so that he could receive the firstborn's blessing. Esau wanted to kill him for that, and Jacob had to run away from home to survive.[2] He ended up living with his uncle. That doesn't sound like a peaceful and functional family to me. Does it to you?

Jacob's life in his new location wasn't much better. Today we tend to look down on someone who has children by multiple partners, yet that describes Jacob. He had children by four different women. And these four women were in constant competition with one another, a characteristic they passed down to their children. The twelve sons were guilty of betrayal,[3] adultery,[4] and murder.[5] Their sibling rivalry was so bad that it prompted them to sell the brother Jacob loved most into slavery. That sounds pretty dysfunctional, doesn't it?

What was Jacob doing while his wives and concubines, along with their children, were creating this chaos? Mostly he was working. He was a classic third-base runner. He spent most of his time building his career and his fortune. By working hard and building his flocks, he became very wealthy. Genesis 30:43 says, "In this way the man grew exceedingly prosperous and came to own large flocks, and female and male servants, and camels and donkeys."

No Comfort

Jacob had just about every material thing a person could want during his era. He had God's favor. He had wealth. He had respect. He had numerous children and grandchildren, signs of blessing during his time. Despite all these things, he was not content. Why? Because his family relationships were so broken.

When his eleven sons lied to him and told him that Joseph was dead,

Jacob was devastated. The formula of worldly success plus God's favor was not greater than the pain of broken relationships. When Jacob was told Joseph was dead, here is how the father responded: "Then Jacob tore his clothes, put on sackcloth and mourned for his son many days. All his sons and daughters came to comfort him, but he refused to be comforted. 'No,' he said, 'I will continue to mourn until I join my son in the grave.' So his father wept for him."[6] Neither his wealth nor God's favor nor the attempts of others to comfort him could salve the wound or resolve the sorrow of losing someone he loved.

All of Jacob's successes meant nothing to him as he grew older. Even twenty years after the loss of Joseph, he was still feeling the effects of it. Joseph's brothers were also still feeling it. When they visited Egypt to buy food and they unknowingly encountered Joseph, Reuben said, "Didn't I tell you not to sin against the boy? But you wouldn't listen! Now we must give an accounting for his blood."[7] As soon as they experienced trouble, the *first* thing that came to mind was what they had done to Joseph. Time had not healed that wound.

Ironically, when the brothers sold Joseph into slavery, they thought removing Joseph would bring them closer to their father. Instead, it drove him farther away. Every day of their lives, the deception about Joseph must have been like an elephant in the room. Every day of their lives, they must have thought about it. Jacob's sorrow was probably always just under the surface, ready to break through as it did on the day his sons came home from Egypt without Simeon and saying that they were required to take Benjamin back there with them.

"You have deprived me of my children," Jacob scolded. "Joseph is no more and Simeon is no more, and now you want to take Benjamin. Everything is against me!...My son will not go down there with you; his brother is dead and he is the only one left. If harm comes to him on the journey you are taking, you will bring my gray head down to the grave in sorrow."[8]

What lesson could God teach us from the story of Jacob's family?

What if God is trying to show us that if we don't get second-base relationships right, our lives will be full of sorrow? Only after Joseph and his brothers talked about what had happened was forgiveness given all around; only after they saw things from God's perspective was their family able to begin healing.

The Elephant in the Room

Leaving relational problems unresolved is like living every day with an elephant in the room. I'm guessing that you're familiar with this common metaphor. The idea suggests that if a real elephant were standing in the room, it would be so obvious and absurdly out of place that it would *have* to be the topic of discussion. Ignoring the elephant and leaving it unaddressed would require everyone to pretend not to see it. How absurd! An elephant is enormous. If it were in a room, it would not only be in the way, but it would also stink up everything in the room. It would be impossible to live with a real elephant in your home and pretend that everything is normal.

Yet many families do this all the time. Someone in our world is physically or verbally abusive, does drugs, gets drunk, hoards, steals, spends uncontrollably, or exhibits some other destructive behavior, and everyone else pretends nothing wrong is happening. They ignore the problem and hope it will go away. But that doesn't work. And if someone from outside that dysfunctional world points out the elephant, we say, "Elephant? What elephant? I don't see an elephant." We put on a phony face. We become less authentic with others and start living in a world of pretense. We compensate for the elephant in the room. We say everything is fine, but at our core we're conflicted because our relationships are suffering, and so are we. Our families become crippled by the problems we refuse to deal with as the dysfunction grows and we are silent.

Not long ago, I did a sermon series about the Fine family. You probably know these types of people. Ask how they're doing, and the answer is, "Fine." How is your marriage? "Fine." How are your kids doing? "Fine." The problem is that they aren't really fine. They have an elephant in the room, but instead of dealing with it, they make it into the family pet. That's why we handed out window clings for people's cars during the sermon series that looked like this:

The Fine Family

I still see people driving around town with these clings on the back windows of their cars.

I did the series because too many people pretend they don't have problems—especially people in churches. But everyone has problems. And every family has issues to deal with. The question is whether we're going to deal with them. Healthy families address the elephant in the room and work through their dysfunction. Ironically, it's usually the family who is willing to confess they are not fine and work through things that turns out to actually become fine. They become whole when they become an elephant-free family.

John's Perspective

All healthy relationships are based on truth and trust. For a relationship to be solid, people need to be honest with one another. That doesn't just mean being honest about yourself. It means being honest with others. Ephesians 4:15 admonishes us to speak the truth in love to one another. We cannot control the response of another person or the outcome of honest conversation. But if we honestly put issues on the table with others and attempt to resolve them in a Christ-like way, we give ourselves the best chance of building strong, honest, healthy relationships.

Healing for Jacob's Family

How did Jacob's family finally become more stable and able to function relationally? One person got healthy and was willing to talk about the elephant in the room. That person was Joseph. When he was a teenager telling his family about his visions of superiority, he was arrogant and selfish. Though he may not have been aware of it, he really thought everything was about him. He wanted and expected to be served by everyone in his family.

Slavery in Egypt taught him humility. It also helped him learn to serve others. It's difficult to be arrogant when you are a slave—a piece of property. First in Potiphar's house and then in the prison, he learned to give God the glory, to be patient, and to see life from others' point of view. He allowed himself to be broken and rebuilt according to God's priorities. He learned how to win at home plate and first base. And decades later when he finally got a chance to see his family again, he spoke up about the elephant in the room, saying,

I am your brother Joseph, the one you sold into Egypt! And now, do not be distressed and do not be angry with yourselves for selling me here, because it was to save lives that God sent me ahead of you. For two years now there has been famine in the land, and for the next five years there will be no plowing and reaping. But God sent me ahead of you to preserve for you a remnant on earth and to save your lives by a great deliverance.[9]

Healthy people with God-strengthened character talk about their issues. They don't pretend. They don't hide. They don't run away from healthy confrontation. They don't avoid their problems and hope they will go away. They address them and work hard to resolve them. Dealing with your own character issues and depending on God gives you confidence to tackle relational issues.

How might your life change if you talked about the elephant in the room so that you could live with elephant-free relationships? What if that is what needs to be done to put your family or other important relationships on the road to healing and restoration? That's not easy. We don't like to be vulnerable. We don't like to be wrong. We don't like to say we're sorry and ask forgiveness. Yet if we have relational problems, these are things we need to do. We must overcome our natural inclination toward pretense, identify our problems, and humbly work at addressing our part in them.

How to Win Second Base

An attitude of humility and a willingness to change are huge if we want to be successful at the community base. But what must we do specifically to build relationships? That's a difficult question, because there are so many different kinds of relational problems with so many root causes, resulting in all kinds of brokenness. It's a little bit like the field of medicine. How many different kinds of sickness are there? How many specialties are there? There are even specialties within specialties. Making a complicated matter even more difficult is the fact that the longer you've been broken, the more complicated your injury is to heal. How in the world can a book like this help with such a complicated problem?

John's Perspective

Do you know how the government trains Treasury agents to recognize counterfeit money? Believe it or not, they don't study counterfeits. They study the real thing. Agents spend countless hours examining and handling real bills so that they become totally familiar with them.

If you have a troubled background or difficulties with relationships, then you need to be around healthy people. You need to become familiar with what's right and normal so that you have models you can emulate.

I'm not going to try to diagnose and address the different kinds of brokenness. Instead I'll offer suggestions for how to train for relational health and fitness. Just as all good programs promoting physical fitness have a few essential actions in common—eat right, stay active, drink lots of water, and get an adequate amount of sleep—a sound program promoting good relationships requires a few basic things. Here are four that I believe to be essential.

1. Value Others More than Yourself

God built us for community. We are designed to be in relationships. But the reality of natural selfishness due to sin derails even the best of intentions. We need to recognize that and deal with it appropriately.

When I married Marcia on August 7, 1982, I promised to love her. That was an easy vow to make, because I felt it strongly and expected it to grow over the years and last for a lifetime. I even had the extra motivation of coming from a broken home, so I was determined to make marriage work. But after just two years together, I wondered how my parents had made it for sixteen. I often found myself thinking, *Wow, I married a stubborn and selfish woman.* And guess what she was thinking: *Wow, I married a stubborn, selfish man!*

Most married couples have thought such things about their spouse. Most family members have thought that about other family members. Friends think that about other friends. It's normal, but it's not helpful. And my thinking about Marcia threatened to blow up our marriage—unless something changed.

What needed to change? My mind. How did I need to change? Philippians 2:1–4 says, "If you have any encouragement from being united with Christ...then make my joy complete by being like-minded, having the same love, being one in spirit and of one mind. Do nothing out of selfish ambition or vain conceit. Rather, in humility value others above yourselves, not looking to your own interests but each of you to the interests of the others." I knew these words. I had read these teachings many times. And I believed them. I just wanted Marcia to be the one to practice them first! Don't we all expect that of our spouses?

But then something happened. We had another argument and I lost my temper again. But this time I raised my hand as if threatening to hit her. She just looked at me steely-eyed and said, "Go ahead, *Pastor*, hit me."

I didn't, and I never have. But in that moment I realized that I could not blame my temper on anyone else—not my father's modeling, not my wife's antagonism. I needed to own my selfishness and grow up if I wanted to win in my marriage and my other relationships.

Added to that incident was finally understanding Ephesians 5:21 as if for the first time: "Submit to one another out of reverence for Christ." Somehow God got my attention with this verse and used it to transform my thinking about relationships. I had been perpetually caught in a battle of the wills in my marriage and with others. But this verse helped me start to look at my marriage in a new way. I imagined a triangle with God at the top and with Marcia and me at each of the two corners. If I would attend to submitting to God first and drawing near him, then I would move up the triangle. As Marcia did the same, she would move up the triangle. And here's the insight God gave that was simple and profound. The closer we got to God, the closer we got to each other.

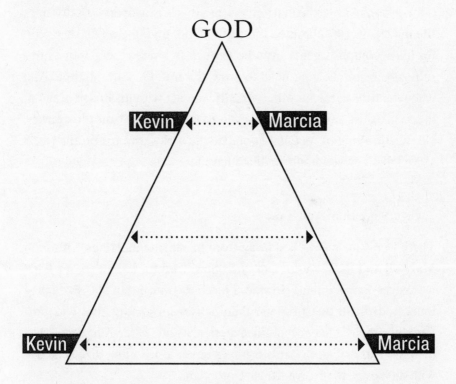

The idea is *mutual voluntary submission.* I had to put Marcia ahead of myself and serve her without waiting for her to serve me first. I had to submit to her. She had to do the same with me. We discovered in our marriage that if we could make God our focus and possess a mind-set of submission to God and our spouse, we could close the gaps among all three of us. That has been Marcia's and my recipe for first saving and then building and sustaining our marriage.

This concept of *mutual voluntary submission* out of reverence for Christ changed everything for me. It impacted every relationship in my life. It changed how we did marriage. It changed how I led my church board. It changed how I treated the staff. It changed how I went after team leadership. I no longer had to fight for myself. I submitted to God and tried to value others in the way that God values me. It was life changing.

You don't have to be married to learn this lesson or apply it. Joseph's life models it. He submitted himself to God, giving God all the credit for his accomplishments. And he learned to value others above himself. As a result, he continued to grow closer to God all the time. And when the time came for him to finally interact with his brothers again, he wasn't thinking of revenge, even though it was within his power. He was thinking of reconciliation. He drew closer to his brothers and served them even though he didn't have to.

2. Give More than You Take

There were times I walked away from mentoring meetings with John Maxwell and I felt, well, there's no other word for it than *stupid*. That was never John's intent. He would listen to what I thought was a profoundly difficult question and then deliver an answer that was profoundly simple. That's what life experience and leadership success has the power to deliver. It can sift issues down to a Twitter-size sentence with the power to resolve life-size problems.

During one session with John, I was wrestling with major relationship problems. I was frustrated by the give-and-take of relationships. I was wondering how you keep the score even, and how to keep others from taking advantage. That's when he offered this million-dollar insight: "Always give more than you take."

I know that may not sound profound. Maybe that's because it's so much easier to say than to live. But I've watched John practice it over and over, particularly with his wife, Margaret. He made it look so simple. So I vowed to try to do the same, to try to give more than I take, moment-to-moment, day-to-day.

If you want to do this, my advice is to start with the little things. I can illustrate how with a bagel. Here's what I mean: Every seven days I take Thursday as my day off. (Remember, pastors work weekends.) Many Thursdays, Marcia and I would drop Jadon off at school and then head to the fitness club together for a workout. But before the workout, we'd stop at a bagel shop to split a ham, egg, and cheese bagel on honey whole wheat and a cinnamon bagel with honey almond cream cheese.

Each time Marcia would sit down at the table and I would pick up the bagels at the counter. As I walked to the table, I would eye the bagels to figure out which was the better half—the bigger one, the one with more cinnamon and sugar; you get the idea. Then I would joyfully put the better halves on Marcia's napkin without comment or fanfare.

That's it. It's too simple. But the majority of relationship problems could be solved by such simple decisions. Give someone else the better half. Look after someone else's interests instead of your own. When you do this in life, relationships work. When you don't—relationships break down. We all tend to take more than we give, and that creates problems.

One of the lessons John has taught that has been woven into my life is the idea of adding value to others. I've watched his commitment to it, and it has made a deep impression on me.

John's Perspective

For as long as I can remember, I've cared about people. But I didn't always know to add value to them. Early in my career, I was more concerned with accomplishing my vision than I was with helping

(Continued)

others. My thinking was, *How can I get people to help me with my agenda?* But then I realized that was the wrong way to think. Instead I focused on helping people. And I discovered that if I added value to others first, then they would also add value to me.

As I matured in my leadership, I also discovered that the best way to develop one's leadership was to develop other leaders, which is just another way of adding value. Whether I'm interacting with a family member, a friend, an employee, a client, or a customer, my goal is always to add value, give more, and do it first. When I do that and worry less about the return, the relationship improves and everybody wins.

Your life and mine are filled with bagel moments at home, in business, at the church, and on the ball field. In those moments, we can choose to add value to others. When you are faced with those moments, what will you do? Will you take more than you give, or give more than you take? If you do the latter, it will change your life.

3. Forgive What We Can't Forget

Everyone has been disappointed, let down, or hurt by other people. The more important that person is to you, the greater and deeper the pain usually is. Further, this world is full of injustice, and most of us have endured indignity at someone else's hand. It's unlikely that you can reach your twenties without receiving some scars from family and friends. The question is: What do you do with those things? Do you keep score? Do you nurse grudges? Do you focus on the pain, or do you work to forgive others and release yourself from the toxic waste of bitterness?

As you can probably guess, the most difficult pain I have had to overcome and forgive came from the breakup of my family. When I was a toddler, my parents came to faith in Christ. So during my elementary education years, one of the places that was important in my life was church. The church we attended had between one and two hundred people, and my dad was among the lay leaders. So when I was age four to ten, Dad talked about God and the Bible, and he expected us to embrace the values he espoused.

At the same time, something was not quite right. Soon enough his temper seemed to take center stage, and we were expected to be quiet and walk on eggshells. We learned to live with an elephant in the room.

After the divorce, Dad progressively dismissed me. He'd say words like, "Love you, son," but his actions proved his words hollow. When the family split up, we went from kind of poor to flat-out poor. I watched my uneducated mom struggle mightily to provide for us. Meanwhile, I took on emotional responsibilities that should have been my dad's. Feelings of rejection, abandonment, and powerlessness settled deep within me and became my new normal. I will never forget how it felt to use food stamps, live in government-subsidized housing, and rely on the kindness of others to survive. My relationship with Dad withered to nothing. When we had occasional encounters, he'd talk like a dad, but there was no real relationship. And I started to resent him.

I was determined to make something of myself, so I went to college a year early as a seventeen-year-old. College was a rough season. I was going to school full-time, volunteering at a church, and working twenty hours a week. But I still fell short financially. I needed $500 or I was going to be out of college. I'd become desperate, so desperate that when I came home one weekend, I humbled myself to ask my dad for a loan.

"Dad, I need $500 or I'm going to have to leave college," I said. "I don't have money for the bills or food or rent. Can you help me?"

He had picked me up in his brand-new Lincoln Mark V, something his new wife had bought because she had some money.

"Well, son," he said, "she has the money, so no, I can't help you. But you can ask her."

I was stunned. "Ask her?" *She's not my mom*, I thought. *I don't even know her. You're supposed to be my dad. You still work. I'm asking for help from you, not her.*

"Son, she controls the money and you'll have to ask her."

Well, I swallowed my pride some more and went to her for the loan. My dad never did help. A few years later, he bought my sister a sports car when she was sixteen. Meanwhile I struggled in college without transportation and often had only twenty-five cents to buy a box of mac and cheese to survive.

I realized in that season that there was an elephant in the room and I did not want to admit it. The truth was that my dad loved himself, but he did not love me. I had felt like I was on my own to figure out how to become a man since I was in my early teens. I then realized I was on my own for life. Though he was my biological father, he did not care enough to do anything for me. That was something I carried with me every day, and it negatively impacted all of my relationships.

In my late twenties, I was a full-time pastor, married with two children. Having become a father, I was confounded by my father's choices to disconnect from me. Then one day my father called me on the phone. We hadn't talked in years.

"Son," he accused, "you have no idea what it's like to be a grandpa and not know your grandkids!"

"You are correct," I answered. "I do not. And God helping me, I never will. Because having become a father, I do not know how you could throw away a relationship with me, your son. You emotionally disengaged, took the only other two men in the family [my brothers], and left me. You did not help as I tried to become a man, as I worked through college and rose to become a pastor. You have major issues, as your imprisonment would indicate, and I don't know what you want in this phone call. But if you want a relationship with your grandkids, it will come only if you restore a relationship with me first. You won't bring that elephant into our home. So start with me, not with them!"

As you might guess, he never chose to do anything about that. He might tell you differently. We all have our own perspective on life.

What did I learn from all this? I cannot hold on to resentment or it will wreck my relationships. I cannot carry bitterness or it will contaminate my spirit. I cannot take revenge or it will twist me into embracing deception. I cannot demand justice because I am in such need of God's mercy and grace myself in my life. So all I can do is release these things to God, and forgive what I cannot forget.

I forgave my father by the time I was in my early thirties. He had not asked for it, but knowing that Christ has forgiven me for all the wrongs I have done, what else could I do? It wasn't until I entered into a mentoring relationship with John, however, that I realized what someone looked like who had no baggage of bitterness. At first, I was skeptical. I thought there must be something. Without John's knowing it, I investigated how he dealt with so many people in life and ministry who vomited their anger, betrayed his trust, stole from him, or lied to him. I found nothing. What was his secret? Again, it was simple: "Keep short accounts."

John's advice was pure gold. I cannot tell you how it changed everything in my life. Before, I had kept score with everyone. Now I let things go. Why is that so important? People who keep short accounts don't carry a wounded spirit, so they are not easily hurt. They don't lash out. They trust and keep adding value to others. Curiously, they end up living freer than others!

I wish I could give this gift to you: *Let it go, forget about it, and what you cannot forget, just forgive!* It will change *all* your relationships. And if you've done wrong to others, repent and ask them for forgiveness.

A few years ago, a man in my congregation came to me and said, "I've heard the stories you've told about your family growing up. To some degree, what your dad did in blowing up your family and abandoning you, I have done to my family and kids. I have so much regret, what do I do?"

I gave him the same advice: repent. "That's where you need to start," I said. "Go to each of your children. Authentically repent. Humbly seek their forgiveness. You can't control their response, but you can confess your regret. And if you are sincere, you can begin to change." Where there is forgiveness, there is always hope for repairing a broken relationship.

4. Let God Change People

What if you do everything right in a relationship, yet it still goes wrong? Many people try to change or fix the other person. That usually doesn't work. In fact, it can make the relationship worse by creating co-dependency. So what do you do? Put the other person in God's hands. Changing people is God's responsibility, not yours.

Joseph's brothers wanted him to change. When he didn't, they took matters into their own hands. They took action, but it was inappropriate action. I imagine that when Joseph was in the pit waiting to be sold into slavery, he was thinking, *What are you doing? You should be bowing to me!*

Joseph did change, but only when he depended on God. And he changed not in the way his brothers wanted, but in the way that God wanted. And ironically, though his brothers wouldn't have chosen the changes that God did, those changes were exactly what the brothers ultimately needed and wanted.

Do you want change? God can do that. But we always need to remember that God takes the long view. He sees the big picture. If we want our way, we often pigeonhole ourselves or others. If you choose to follow God, He will change you. You can't follow Him and remain the same.

If you aren't changing, you need to ask yourself whether you are really following God. If we depend on God and open ourselves up to what He would do, then we will change in ways that only God can anticipate. And He will use those changes for His good.

The same can be said of others. God can change them. And it would serve us well to remember that we don't know better than God does how another person needs to change. We don't know how He will use someone else. We must leave that to God.

John's Perspective

If you're a leader, how do you balance encouraging others, holding them accountable, and allowing God to change them? That's a difficult balance to achieve—especially for an optimistic encourager like me. I see the best in people and think I can help anyone improve. That's both a blessing and a curse. The good news is that I like to help and encourage others. The bad news is that I'm terrible at hiring people because I think everyone can become a great employee. My hiring often created problems for my organizations, so my leaders stopped allowing me to do it.

When it comes to working with employees, I try to encourage everyone. George M. Adams called encouragement "oxygen to the soul." Everybody needs that. But I also try to set clear expectations. Give people clear goals and a deadline if they aren't performing. If they fail to meet those expectations, give them a chance to change. At that point, it's up to them and God. If they won't change, then it's time to make a change.

Finding a Heart for People

Some people seem to be naturally good at developing relationships. People like John Maxwell are masters at it. Others have to work at it. That was the case for a friend named Charlie Wetzel. He arrived at 12Stone a few months after the bus trip. Charlie had been a believer for many years and had come from John Maxwell's church in San Diego, so I encouraged him to jump into ministry. He began working with one of my staff members in the area of small groups, where Charlie had several years of experience.

Not long after Charlie arrived, I remember seeing him at a church event for leaders in which I asked the extroverts in the room to go around to other tables and introduce themselves. When I saw that Charlie didn't get up, I chided him: "What are you doing sitting down? You're an extrovert!"

"No, I'm an introvert," he responded, "but I'll be glad to go introduce myself."

That made me curious to learn Charlie's story. He later told me that he grew up as a shy and self-conscious kid with poor people skills. And he wasn't very self-aware, either. At thirty, he still hadn't gained any traction in life. He tended to bounce from job to job—chef, teacher, college dean. He had a strong work ethic, and he was usually good at the actual work, but his poor people skills often undermined him. He didn't do much better in his personal relationships. He moved from one dysfunctional relationship to another for years.

When he was thirty-one, Charlie moved to California and had a hard time finding a job. He ended up selling cars for almost a year.

"Talk about a stretch!" says Charlie, "I was an introvert who really didn't know a lot about money, and every day I had to talk to strangers who hated me on sight because I was a car salesman, and I had to ask them for tens of thousands of dollars!"

How did he come to sell cars? "I sat in my car arguing with God about applying for that job. I didn't want it, but I knew God wanted me to apply for it. When I got it, I was both happy to have a job and unhappy to have *that* one."

It turned out to be exactly what he needed. Selling cars taught him how to approach strangers, make small talk, ask questions, and really listen to people.

"It's one of the best things that ever happened to me," he now says. "It changed my life. That's where I finally learned how to work with people."

Working as a car salesman was only a start. It changed Charlie's skills, but it didn't really change his heart toward people. That occurred when he was training to become a small group leader in San Diego. Being an apprentice leader really took him out of his comfort zone. His role as a spiritual leader forced him to engage with people on another level.

"A battle used to go on between what I sensed I *should* do and what I wanted to do. I felt I should initiate, connect with people, and go out of my way to help, but internally I was fearful and wanted to hold back," says Charlie. "But there came a moment when I realized that everything God did, He did for people. I could not be a true follower of Christ and not care about people and building relationships. That realization gave me the courage and conviction to change."

Set Up for Success

In baseball, they say when you're on second base you're in scoring position. That can also be said of the people base in God's game plan for living. If you care about people and are capable of developing healthy relationships with them, then you are in position to be successful when it comes to your family, your community, and your career. If an introvert like Charlie who considered himself to have few people skills was able to change, then so can you.

What would happen if you put others ahead of yourself? How would your relationship with your spouse or significant other change? What would happen if you forgave the people who have hurt you in life? How would it change your relationships with family members? How much easier would it be for you to be loving and giving? What would happen if you went out of your way to give more than you take and serve others—and do it from the heart? How would that impact your co-workers and your neighbors?

The answer? It would set you up for success! Like nothing else can, your relationships can be a launching pad for third-base results. You can find out more about that in the next chapter.

John's Application Guide

Discussion Questions

1. What is one of your favorite memories involving people? Describe it. Why is it a favorite?

2. Why do you think that Jacob's family relationships were so dysfunctional? Do you find it comforting to know that someone God used started out where Jacob did? Explain.

3. Up to now, when you have experienced conflict or dysfunction in a relationship, how have you usually responded to it? What would it take for you to follow Joseph's example and develop relationships in a healthier way?

4. The ability to value others more than yourself comes from the heart. How difficult do you find it to do that? Read Romans 12:3–5. What insights can you gain from this Scripture?

5. In what ways do you attempt to give more than you take? In what areas do you find that difficult to do? What must change in you for you to live out that value in every area of life?
6. Do you find it easy or difficult to let God change others instead of trying to change them yourself? Explain.

Assignment

Forgiveness is at the heart of maintaining good relationships in community and winning second base. You must be willing to ask for forgiveness and give it as well. To embrace forgiveness, do the following:

A. **Seek Forgiveness:** Set aside some time to reflect on the ways you have hurt other people, whether intentionally or accidentally. Then make a list of people from whom you should ask forgiveness. Before you approach them, spend time with God asking Him to forgive you and to grant you the grace to forgive yourself. After you have received God's forgiveness, humbly approach each person on your list privately to confess your wrong and ask for forgiveness. If appropriate, offer to try to make things right with the person. Remember, you cannot and should not try to control their response. Many will forgive you. If someone doesn't, you must try to be content with having done the right thing and allowing God to change the person.
B. **Grant Forgiveness:** As Kevin mentioned, everyone has been hurt by others. Spend time reflecting on the hurts you remember that have impacted you negatively. Go back as far in your life as necessary. You may want to write them out in a prayer journal. Once you have brought to mind the hurts,

(Continued)

have a conversation with God about them. Tell Him about your pain, frustration, and disappointment. Cry, shout—do whatever you must to be honest with God. Then ask Him to help you forgive each person—and God—for the emotional, physical, and spiritual hurts you have received. This may take some time. If any people on your list asked you for forgiveness in the past and you declined to give it, then seek them out and tell them that you forgive them.

8

Third Base: How to Win Results

As a rule in our society, people are esteemed for their career and material success. It seems to be true from sports to Hollywood, from politics to business. You can lack character, but if you have cash you'll be envied. If you blow up your marriage but build your career, people call you successful. However, if you build up your marriage and

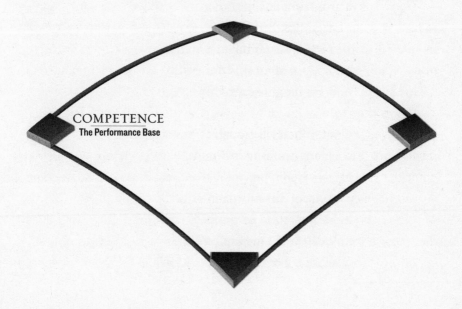

COMPETENCE
The Performance Base

163

family but your work world stalls, people dismiss you. "Nice person," they say, "but hasn't done much." That's why it's important to remember one of life's most transforming truths: God doesn't keep score the way we do. In fact, you'll never have a home run life until you start to see things from God's perspective.

God Likes to Grow Things

So is God anti-success? Is that the conclusion? I don't think anyone can make a valid argument for that. God is the author of success. He is the Creator and He likes to grow things. If you've never thought about it this way before, consider what Genesis tells us: "In the beginning God created the heavens and the earth."[1] Scripture goes on to explain how God created vegetation: plants and trees. He created living creatures each according to their kind. He created human beings. And in us He put the capacity to reproduce. The growth and improvement process is woven into the very fabric of the world.

God likes to grow people, too. Adam and Eve were the only people in history who started life fully formed. Every other person took nine months (give or take) in the womb and eighteen years in the world to grow to adulthood. What if God is using all these things in nature to try to teach us how He likes to *grow* things?

Physical growth as children was automatic for all but a few of us. However, every other kind of growth is optional. God shows us how it can work, and He invites us to it. But we have to choose whether or not to accept the invitation. We can resist it, but if we do, we're going against the way results come—through growth.

Let's say you're interested in owning a business. How long does that take to develop? First, you need to know how to create a product or provide a service. That takes time. Malcolm Gladwell suggests that people at the top of their profession require ten thousand hours to develop their skills. A start-up business also needs seed money. Have you ever thought about why people call it that: seed money? Because they know that creating a business is a growth process. The money helps you plant the seed in your business. But you must water, weed, and fertilize before it produces a return.

How long does it take to grow a Super Bowl–winning football team? To answer that, start by looking at the players. If the players' average age is about twenty-five, then it takes those twenty-five years of coaching and leadership to get that person ready to play on the team. It takes the organization decades to finance the team and get it ready to excel. It takes the coaches an entire career to ready themselves to coach. All that happens before the winning season even starts!

In a given season, players and coaches alike must execute through all of training camp, all the pre-season games, and all sixteen regular-season games—just to have the chance to enter the play-offs. Then the team has to win against all the other best teams to have a chance to get into the big game. Do all that, and then they must be able to score more points than the other team, which has fought through a similar process. There is no fast track. It's a long, slow process, and you can't cheat it.

How long does it take to grow a spiritually mature follower of Jesus Christ, someone who produces a return of thirty-, sixty-, or a hundred-fold for the kingdom of God? We want the answer to be days, weeks, or months. The parable of the sower reminds us that God works more slowly. The passage says that some people have a hard heart and may never soften toward God and receive the seed of His truth. Others receive the seed but never put down roots and grow. Others yet take years to develop depth but their growth gets choked out by the weeds of worry or the pursuit of pleasure and wealth. There is one more group that's different, the ones who produce. How long does it take for them to grow, mature, and produce? It takes years or decades. It's never pray and then *poof*—you're mature. It's a slow process of growth.

Even Jesus took time to grow before His life yielded the results for which He came to earth. Once He left eternity, He grew in the womb for nine months. He waited twelve years before He taught in the temple courts. He studied and prepared until age thirty before He began teaching as a rabbi. He selected and trained His twelve disciples for three years before He publicly confessed to be the Messiah. Could Jesus have skipped the whole growth process? Perhaps. But He didn't. Maybe He was trying to teach us something. If God doesn't skip the growth process Himself, why would we expect to skip it?

If we want to become competent in our careers, we need to expect to grow into them. Learning to run the bases the right way takes time and growth. And so does learning how to win at third base. God created us to be in a growth journey for the whole of our lives. As long as you are breathing, you have the potential to grow to a new level. You can learn something. You can train in your talents so that they take you to a new place. You can take your leadership from a five to a six or from an eight to a nine. You can become excellent at your craft. And God desires that you do that. Results matter to Him.

God wants us to grow and succeed, but often we pray asking God to give us a *payoff without the process*. We want to harvest without having to purchase the land, plow the soil, plant the seed, water the plants, weed the soil, feed the plants, and wait until harvest season. Our desires defy the very nature of God's design in creation and us. God wants us to win, but He expects us to grow our skills, develop our talents, and sharpen our leadership competence. He wants us to train.

The question is: Will we give up on the process or grow up into productive people? If you're a recovering workaholic like me, you may be addicted to results. I have to confess that over time I had begun to expect life to be harvest, harvest, harvest when it's designed by God to be plow, plant, harvest. No one's life is harvest, harvest, harvest. The performance base is about *growing* results consistently, not grasping for them instantly.

Raise Your Value

I've written a lot about Joseph in *Home Run* because I've learned so much from him. One of the things that is clear to me is that it took years of growth for Joseph to be ready to fulfill his purpose. When he was a kid, his dream loomed large. By the time he had been in Egypt for a decade, maybe he had lost sight of his dream, had forgotten all about it. But God hadn't forgotten it. Through the years of experiences and trials, God was growing a competent business leader. That takes time. It's always easier to *dream up* something than it is to actually *do* it.

When most of us get an idea—whether it's a vision from God or an idea for a business—we want to take charge and put the idea into practice. When Joseph dreamed of others bowing, he was ready for it to happen *that day*. When I received God's vision to lead a church, I didn't want to wait or to have anyone else tell me how to do it. I wanted to make it happen. But the reality was that, like Joseph, I wasn't ready to lead. And that's true for most people. If you want to learn your craft, you need to serve somebody else. As a rule, if you're in business you have to make money for someone else before you can make it for yourself. You have to lead under someone else before you can lead others. You need to learn the ropes.

Most of us don't like that. In fact, we're so eager to work for ourselves that we blow up or break down when we are required to work under someone else. We're disappointed because we feel we're not being promoted quickly enough. (By the way, Joseph did well at Poti-phar's house and got *demoted* for his efforts!) We often feel that we don't get enough recognition for our contribution. Many people bail out and try again somewhere else, only to repeat the process. They go from job to job waiting for their job conditions to change, when the reality is that *they* need to change.

John's Perspective

Many years ago, my nephew Troy came to live with Margaret and me for a short time after he finished college. Troy had a strong work ethic, and he wanted to be successful. As he took a job with a mortgage company, he asked what advice I would give a young man just starting out in his career. I suggested he do three things:

- Do more than expected every day. I recommended that he always arrive at work thirty minutes early, eat lunch in half the time allotted, and work thirty minutes after quitting time.
- Do something every day to help the people around him. If he added value to others, he could help his team and win over his co-workers.
- Go the extra mile for the boss. I told him to make an appointment with his boss and let him know that if he needed anything extra done—no matter how menial—he was available to help. And that meant after hours or on the weekend.

Troy took my advice and worked hard. He proved himself in his twenties and rose quickly. By the time he turned thirty, he was already a vice president in the organization.

I experienced career discontent in my twenties. I was called to ministry in high school. Though I would have loved to go straight into ministry, I knew I had to get a degree. So I went to college. When I graduated, I took a job with my longtime friend Wayne Schmidt. Like many people in their twenties, I overvalued my contribution and undervalued what my leader and the environment provided for my success.

One day I read an article that had been written about our church that included an interview with Wayne. The person who wrote the article discussed the success of the church and many of the wonderful things being done in the community, which were occurring under Wayne's leadership. As I read the article, I noticed that many of the accomplishments being cited had been projects that I had led. Yet my name was never mentioned! That really bothered me. So I took out a highlighter and marked everything that I had done, and I then made an appointment to talk to Wayne.

"You see this?" I said. "You didn't do that. I did. And this, too." I went through the article pointing out all the work I had done that Wayne was getting credit for. I was about halfway through when there was a moment that I sensed the Holy Spirit was whispering to me that Wayne was about to fire me. I stopped cold.

"Wayne?" I asked. "Are—are you—are you about to fire me?"

"Yes," he answered.

My own stupidity struck me like a ton of bricks. I felt exposed by my own immaturity. Wayne was leading well, God was giving the church His favor, and I was seeking the credit.

I repented for my pride, my attitude, and my immaturity—not only to Wayne, but to the church's board. And I apologized. I was wrong. Wayne, in his kindness, forgave me. But it was the start of a great lesson for me, one that it would take me years to learn: It's not about me.

If you're working for someone else, the way things are going may be bothering you the way they bothered me. You may feel underappreciated, unrecognized. You may feel that you are carrying the load. You may believe you're not being promoted or rewarded the way you deserve. But that's where God often puts us so that we can learn and grow!

The value of making someone else successful is all but ignored by most people in our culture. What if your next growth step is to learn how to serve someone else, to make him or her successful, and in the process to grow in your own skill and competence? What if you are to learn how to go to the next level by helping your boss and his or her business go to the next level?

Joseph did that not once, not twice, but three times! He did it in Potiphar's house, he did it in the prison, and then he got the chance to do it for the entire nation. By the time Pharaoh had a dream that no one could figure out, Joseph was thirty years old. For thirteen years he had worked for other people and made them successful. He'd been taking responsibility for creating results since he was seventeen, and he had learned the process so well that he could repeat it wherever he went. Not only that, but when he shared with Pharaoh the interpretation that God had given him, Joseph was savvy enough and experienced enough to also communicate a solution, not just a problem.

Real leaders offer solutions. In the case of Joseph, in one concise conversation, he identified the pending financial crisis about to befall Egypt and simultaneously offered a solution so clear and compelling that it earned him the mother of all promotions: second in command of Egypt. All the people in the world who'd once ruled over him were then working for him.[2] That included Potiphar, his wife, the prison warden, even the chief cupbearer and ultimately his own brothers.

Joseph's solution to the coming crisis may seem obvious to us now, but it wasn't obvious at the time. Nor was the execution of it easy. He had to find a way to set aside enough food in seven years to save an entire nation plus the children of Israel from starvation in another seven years. If God had allowed Joseph to skip the leadership growth process, what would have happened to all those people? But Joseph had raised his value in each of his positions and had become a sought-after player. He was able to save millions because he was willing to serve others instead of only himself and learned in the process.

What might we have already missed in life because of our own impatience? What might we miss in the future if we try to skip the process that God desires for us? The very challenges we face may be preparing us for a better future. So rise up wherever you're working right now and raise your value.

A Sling for a Sword

Maybe you've already passed that growth gate. Maybe you've already learned to work for others and produce results. By the way, even if you work for yourself or you own your own business, you've probably discovered that you still work for someone else—your customers, your employees, or your shareholders. If so, what's next? What's your next step? Maybe you need to take ownership for your leadership and personal growth. Or as I think of it: Maybe you need to get rid of your sling and pick up a sword.

Everyone needs to learn new skills to go to the next level—I do, you do, John does. This truth came alive to me when I looked at the life of David. What is he most famous for? Killing Goliath. Even people who've never opened a Bible know the story of David and Goliath. The boy used a sling to take down the giant.

Using a sling was something David was really good at. He'd spent years as a shepherd honing his skill with the weapon. And it was a legitimate weapon of war in his day. Scripture speaks of seven hundred Benjamites who could hit a hair with a slung stone without missing it.[3]

David was an expert with the sling. It was comfortable for him. It was familiar. It had brought him success. It had earned him a reputation as a giant killer. But was it the weapon of a future king? Would it help him defeat armies? Would it inspire his warriors to fight and conquer the nation's enemies? No. A sling could never take down the tens of thousands that the nation of Israel would sing about. That would require a sword. It would mean learning a difficult new skill. David was willing to do that. In fact, Scripture never mentions his using a sling again after his defeat of Goliath.

David's willingness to learn and to pay the price for growth was a pattern in his life. As a boy overseeing the flocks for his father, he learned to fight wild animals with his bare hands.[4] Despite having that ability, he still taught himself to use the sling and became an expert with it. And even though he had skill with the sling, he learned the art of swordsmanship. David reinvented himself over and over. He was anointed to be king at the age of thirteen, but he spent the next seventeen years learning to lead. At age thirty, he was finally crowned king of Judah, and he spent nearly eight more years leading and fighting until he reigned over all of Israel.

Perhaps the greatest growth lesson we can learn from David is a willingness to lay down a sling for a sword. Maybe you've mastered a skill that has helped you to get results at your current level and God is inviting you to learn something new, to pick up a sword! God had more for David; He had put more in him. But David had to be willing to do more training and learn a new weapon. Maybe you've taken down a Goliath, but God wants you to conquer tens of thousands. Are you willing to give up your comfortable sling for the potential that comes from the uncomfortable sword? Are you willing to trade what you know for what you don't know?

I've had to do this over and over in my career. It's the price my colleagues and I have to pay to grow and improve our results. For example, I used to know everyone in my church, and I liked it that way. It was comfortable. Why was it a problem? Because you can't grow and reach more people if you insist on knowing everyone personally. If you're a pastor and God has called you to reach more than two hundred people, you have to give that up and learn new skills.

Another example can be seen in how messages are presented. Growing up in church, we used flannel graphs to illustrate messages. You may not be old enough to even know what those are! When that stopped connecting with people, we had a choice: Keep using it, stop using it and do nothing in its place, or learn new skills. When we planted 12Stone, we started using live drama. There's a steep learning curve for doing that well. Then when our world shifted more and more to watching screens—television, movies, video games, YouTube—we realized we had to learn how to do video and film. That learning curve is even steeper.

When our staff grew large, I had to give up leading everyone on the team directly and bring in an executive pastor. That was uncomfortable. When our building got full, we had to learn how to do multiple services. That was exhausting. When the services started to fill up, we learned how to lead multiple campuses. That also meant learning additional sets of skills for communicating remotely via movie screens. Learning to speak to a live audience and a camera at the same time has been a demanding process. There is no end to the need for growth.

We keep trading a sling for a sword in area after area. If we want to reach people, that's what we have to do. You may be tempted to just opt out of this whole process in your profession. I guess we could, too. Many churches have. Some leaders won't change because it's so difficult. Others rationalize that the old ways are somehow better, more righteous, more holy. I'm glad the original church didn't think that way. The church of Acts didn't have Bibles. If later believers had insisted that the old way was the only way and had been unwilling to grow, the New Testament never would have been compiled and *we* wouldn't have Bibles today.

I find it hard to lay down a sling for a sword. But the only other choice is to stall. If David had been unwilling to learn how to fight with a sword, that first battle with Goliath, which he had at age seventeen, might have been his last battle. His best years would have already been behind him. In his twenties, he would have been talking about his memories of past glory, not dreams of God's future. But David did pick up a sword. And I see no evidence that David talked much about Goliath or his battle with him after the fact. He was looking forward and changing to meet future challenges.

John's Perspective

What's the greatest enemy of tomorrow's success? Today's success. Why? Because what got you there won't keep you there.

If you want to reach your potential, you must become a lifelong learner. You must dedicate yourself to personal growth in your areas of greatest strength. What were David's greatest strengths? Fighting, leadership, and worship. So what did he focus his attention on developing? As Kevin said, David learned how to become a skilled warrior. He also continued to improve his leadership so that he could unite and lead the entire nation of Israel. And the evidence of his skill as a musician and songwriter can be found in the book of Psalms.

What skills do you need to develop? I focus most of my third-base effort on leadership and communication. Those are my greatest strengths. What are yours? You need to stay in your strength zone but get out of your comfort zone. Do what's necessary to keep learning and growing to the next level.

Major-League Mentoring

As I've already written, John helped me tremendously at second base. Up through my thirties, I carried a lot of relational baggage. John helped me to lay it down, to cease collecting wrongs, and stop keeping score with other people. As soon as my relational vision cleared, my focus shifted to third base as I sought more help with career questions.

I remember an early conversation with John in which he said, "Kevin, the power of vision is in how deep it's in you, in the art of how you say it, in how often you say it, and in the stories that carry it. But vision leaks. And mostly, it leaks in leaders. Leaders talk about change and growth as if they value it, but they are the least likely to change."

It became clear to me that if I wanted to do what God was calling me to, I'd have to make a deep commitment to growth. As I wrote down what John said—which, by the way, I always do when we meet—I made a note to myself that I have come back to often. It says, "This year, this month, this week, this day, do I still agree to grow?"

I have the same question for you: Do you agree to grow? Are you willing to keep growing? It's the only way to win at third base.

To help you, I'm going to share four of the dozens of lessons John has taught me during our mentoring sessions. These insights helped me to grow at third base. My hope is that reading this will be like having John mentor you.

1. Bring *Your* Talent to the Table

How do you judge your third-base level of competence? How do you know where you stand when it comes to career performance? Most of us compare ourselves with other people and how they're doing. I believe that's one of the worst things you can do to yourself professionally. God does not create everyone the same, nor does He provide a level playing field for everyone, yet somehow that's what we seem to expect.

The parable of the talents in Scripture makes it clear that God doesn't treat everyone equally. To some people God gives five, to others two, to others one talent.[5] It's God's prerogative to distribute His gifts any way He desires. And the parable of the ten minas (coins) makes it clear that even when people are given equal resources, the outcomes are different.[6] Some earn five more, some two, and some none for their master. Even the way the master handles the servants creates jealousy. When He gives another mina to the one who already has ten, others object. As human beings, we seem to have a hard time with the idea that everything isn't equal.

The disciples fell into this comparison game. James and John wanted to be elevated above their peers. They wanted to be seated at Jesus's right and left hand in His glory.[7] The other disciples became angry when they learned about this—maybe because they hadn't the courage to ask first! The disciples wanted to gain favor and position over one another. Jesus wanted them to serve each other.

What ended up happening to James and John probably doesn't seem fair to most of us, either. James died early. He didn't get to write a Gospel or a letter to the church. Just as the big mission started, he was martyred for his faith. And what about John, the disciple Jesus loved? He ended up as an old man in exile, the last of the disciples, living in a cave on the island of Patmos and writing the book of Revelation.

These brothers wanted to be the greatest of the apostles. Yet some say both their contributions were eclipsed by Paul, who became preacher to the nations and wrote more books of the New Testament than any other person. And Paul wasn't even one of the original twelve. That doesn't seem fair.

It's easy to get caught up in this comparison game, yet it serves no useful purpose. I remember in the years when John Maxwell first began mentoring me, I arrived to meet with him one day and out of the room came Andy Stanley, whom John was also mentoring, from the previous meeting.

It's very tempting for me to compare myself to Andy. His church, North Point Community Church, is across town from mine. Andy started it eight years after I started 12Stone. North Point had been established for only thirteen months when they bought property. Less than a year after that, in 1996, Andy opened a building with a twenty-seven-hundred-seat auditorium. (That's larger than the auditorium we built in 2008.) More than two thousand people showed up the first day their building opened. A year later, four thousand people were attending their church. Compare that with the story I've told you of how 12Stone started.

As John and I talked over lunch that day, I was musing, "How do you explain that kind of growth at North Point? How do they become a church of several thousand?" In the course of John's comments, he said, "Andy simply got to the airport before you."

I was caught off guard. I didn't even know what John meant. "Kevin, here's the deal: North Point is a God-thing just like 12Stone. And Andy got to the airport and left on the plane before you and he's arrived at a church of thousands before you. But God has you on a later flight. So you'll get to the airport in God's time and take your flight. And then you'll arrive at a church of thousands. So celebrate North Point, but *bring your talent to the table.*"

I have never forgotten the lesson. God doesn't compare 12Stone with North Point. He created both of them for His Kingdom work and uses each uniquely. And God doesn't compare me with Andy or anyone else. Neither does God compare you with anyone else.

So, whatever talent we have—great or small, emerging or highly developed—we need to bring it to the table in service to God. Sure, when it comes to business or sports we live in a competitive culture. But if you get preoccupied by or consumed with someone else's talents, you end up excusing yourself from training to develop your own. We can't worry about what we don't have. Neither can we worry about how others treat us. In fact, good leaders don't treat everyone the same anyway. They give the most productive people the most time, money, and resources. God does that. Jesus did that. He valued everyone equally, but He treated everyone differently. If that was good enough for Him, then it should be good enough for us.

2. Don't Let Your Failure Be Final

Once the church started growing and John had been mentoring me, he invited me to speak at a leadership conference in El Paso, Texas. The message he asked me to teach is the concept contained in *Home Run*, about running the bases of life the right way. It was something I had taught to my congregation and had used to develop businesspeople. As I prepared for the conference, I was given advice about how to deliver it by one of the organizers. Though he was not a communicator and it went against my instincts, I took his advice.

November 21, 2000, is a day I will never forget. With great anticipation, I stood before an audience of hundreds—and failed miserably. It was like I took three big swings and whiffed every time. I was "out," but I couldn't leave the playing field. I had to keep talking until my time was up.

Now remember, I speak for a living. I had been in front of thousands of people. I was used to speaking multiple times a week and had been for many years. It's not like I had no experience. I'd been up to bat as a speaker and I knew how to hit that ball. But that day I failed. I felt like I was in a black hole. Without a doubt, it was one of my more notable public humiliations!

I did manage to get to the end of my material, but nothing had connected. I had never experienced anything like it before. I knew I hadn't helped anyone in the room. Just as bad, I'd let John down. Can you even imagine how devastating it would be to have your mentor sitting there while you added embarrassment instead of adding value to him? Ugh! That was the longest forty-five minutes of my life.

On the plane ride home, I knew I would have to sit across from John and face the music. I wanted to crawl under a rock and disappear. But instead of criticizing me, John used it as a teaching moment. He explained how to get out of such a black hole in communication when you find yourself trapped there. He encouraged me to grow from the experience, and he never held it against me—never even brought it up again.

I was blown away by John's kindness in that situation. I would not have been so gracious. At that time in my life, I would have been more concerned with any damage done to my reputation for putting a bad speaker on the platform than with teaching a younger man how to learn from his mistake. I've never forgotten that. More important, I've learned from it.

When I got home, I wrote John a note. In part it said,

You trusted me to deliver teaching that would change people's lives. I love to communicate. I was honored to partner. What a time to crash and burn…What can I say? I have no recourse, no way to make it up to you. I regret that people will not receive what would in fact revolutionize the way they do life and business. The diamond would've been a win for lives to come. This will pain me the most…people lose. In close second is the dereliction of trust with your name. While I always knew someday I would speak alongside you, I never thought that I would be writing this note. You were kind to make light of my failure and offer insight that in fact was my missing piece for recovery. Nonetheless, I am not unaware of the cost of what just occurred.

In the note I enclosed a check for the amount of honorarium I had received. I couldn't in good conscience keep it. I closed by saying,

> Thanks for the mentoring and the growth you have added to my life. I am a better Kingdom player for your influence.

John has talked about turning failure into success. He's written a book called *Failing Forward: Turning Your Mistakes into Stepping Stones for Success*. But it wasn't until that day that I knew that John lived those principles and was willing to pay a price for them.

Months after my failure in El Paso, John invited me to speak again. This time it would be at the Catalyst Conference in October 2001. And the subject of the talk? The same message about running the bases for a home run life. In the lead-up to the conference, you can believe I felt pressure. We all have to manage our failures and shortcomings. I had not lost confidence in my ability to communicate, but you better believe I was very aware of the possibility of failure. I was determined not to allow my El Paso failure to become final.

The night before I was to speak, I experienced one of those curious moments with God. He reassured me that what I was about to do would please Him. And when I spoke the next day, it was an extraordinary speaking experience. God used the teaching to awaken others to a new perspective on life and how they run the bases. They were so moved, the room erupted into a standing ovation. I knew it had nothing to do with me, and everything to do with God kindly demonstrating that failure is not final.

If you desire to do anything of value in life, you will fail. How will you manage that? How will you treat your wounds? What will you do with the chances you get after you fall down and fall short? Don't allow your failures to become final. Learn from it when you strike out and get back in the game.

3. Earn Your Keep Every Day

A budding entrepreneur opened a cleaning business in a small city. She was a hard worker, and like other businesspeople in her community, she was always competing for business. It wasn't long before she became aware of the reputation of one wealthy lady in town who used any particular cleaning service only once. In all her years, she'd never hired the same service twice to clean her large house.

"When I finally got my call," the entrepreneur said, "I was going to give it my personal best. And we went into that home and we cleaned and we gave it our absolute best. As we cleaned throughout the house, we'd find a variety of change along the way, we'd just place it in a little cup in the kitchen."

After completing the job, the entrepreneur received her payment, and left.

Imagine her shock when a few weeks later, she got a phone call from the wealthy lady asking her to clean her house a second time. For the life of her, she couldn't understand why she was getting a second chance when no one else did.

"I would love to do it again," the entrepreneur answered, "but can I ask you a question? With all the people who've cleaned your house, why are you letting me do it a second time?"

"It's very simple," the wealthy lady answered. "One dollar and sixty-one cents."

"Excuse me?"

"You were the only one who found the entire $1.61 in change that I had strategically placed throughout the house," she explained. "Some people found eighty-nine cents. Some found ninety. Some found $1.25. One found $1.40. But you were the only one who found the entire $1.61."

What kind of person are you? If you are a $1.61 person, you will always have a job, you will do well, and you will continue to receive opportunities to move up to higher leagues of play in your career.

We take too much for granted in our culture. More and more people think someone else owes them a job. Others believe that because they were able to deliver in the job at some time in the past that they deserve to keep their job in the present. But the truth is that we need to earn our keep every day. We need to be $1.61 today, and tomorrow, and every day we come to work. People don't pay us for what we did last year, last month, or last week. We need to perform every day, wherever we find ourselves that day. That's what Joseph did, even though he found himself in slavery in Egypt. That's what Daniel did, even though he was in captivity in Babylon. That's what I've observed in John as he's sought to add value to people over the years.

One of the most powerful life lessons I've learned from John's mentoring has been unspoken. John has allowed me to travel with him on many occasions. Sometimes he spoke in a boardroom. Other times to a crowd of hundreds to thousands. In every case that group or company was counting on John to deliver. And each time I observed him, this man who was already highly successful treated the next moment as if it were the most important of his career. John would pour into the people in that boardroom or the audience with his very best. I never saw him rely on his last "at-bat" to give him permission to take the next swing casually.

I took note of his willingness to earn his keep every day. It separates steady success from sporadic success. If someone like him—author of seventy-plus books, international developer of leaders, number one leadership guru in the world—was willing to earn his keep every day, then so am I. And you should be, too.

4. Have a Funeral and Get a New Dream

After the Catalyst Conference of 2001, some of our long-term plans for the church were unfolding. Doors were opening for me to travel and speak. I was being approached by editors to write a book. Leaders of other churches were coming to visit. It's not like we were major league, but we were at least out of Little League. The church was on stable ground and growing by a hundred or more a year. And when you've come from where we did in our early years, this was exciting.

Furthermore, Marcia's and my personal life was getting some oxygen. Josh, the oldest of our three kids, was in high school and learning to drive, while the youngest, Jake, was nearly nine. Thank God we were done with the infant and toddler stages of parenting. Sometimes you have to be past something before you can confess how utterly debilitating it is to you. In this season I'd confessed to my wife, "I am just not wired for the first five years of a kid's life. I'm so much better once they become five or six. The older they get, the easier it is for me as a dad." She conceded life was becoming breathable. We were on an upward trend.

During this season, Marcia and I were leading an Atlanta Falcons Bible study with several players and their wives, and the joke became, "If you drink the water you'll become pregnant." Nearly all the women in the group got pregnant at the same time. So they joked that the old couple, meaning us, would have another one. We laughed, but I privately told my friend, then Falcon kicker Jay Feely, "If Marcia got pregnant, it would be supernatural and it would be the death of all my dreams for my forties. So quit saying that—even in jest."

One month later, I was speaking out west, and just before I got on the plane to return home my phone rang. It was Marcia. All she said was "Honey," and I froze.

Years of marriage will do that to you. Somehow you just know. Before she said anything more, I blurted out, "You can't be, we're on birth control that has worked for nine years!"

Yes indeed: my forty-year-old wife was pregnant!

To say that we were not prepared is an understatement. We had given away or thrown away all evidence that we once had infants in the home.

On that flight home I wrote a note to my future child that was filled with joy. But over the next thirty days the emotional cost of starting over began to suffocate me. I knew it would be exhausting. The energy, time, and attention to raise another child seemed impossible to conjure. Plus, we would now have over fifteen years between our oldest and youngest. We would never have an empty nest. I realized I'd be sixty before he graduated from high school.

In my mind, all my plans for my forties began to disappear. Opportunities to speak, Marcia and I traveling together, a more mobile life, freedom, options—they would never happen in light of the new demands of parenting. I was quickly sinking into quiet depression. Of course I could not explain it to anyone else because having a child is supposed to be a celebration, a blessing. I knew this child would be someday, but in those days, it was undoing me. The door had finally opened for a new life dream, and just as quickly it was closing.

When the news became public to the church, they started calling us Abraham and Sarah for having a kid in our old age. I played up the humor and maintained a smile as a good leader should. But privately, I wrote my resignation letter to 12Stone. I can't explain why, but I just could not face my forties starting over. I was a quiet wreck.

When I met John for our next mentoring lunch he congratulated me. I smiled and struggled to hide the depression. But he could sense how I really felt. He knew how deeply I was struggling. Then he spoke the words that still echo: "Kevin, you need to have a funeral and get a new dream."

What John taught me that day was that there is no value in pretending. I had had a dream for my forties that was now dead—as dead as my mom the day cancer finally took her life at age fifty-three.

As dead as my brother the day of his motorcycle accident at age forty-one.

What do you do when someone dies? You have a funeral. What do you do when something inside of you dies? You have a funeral. You take all the emotion and intensity of the loss and face it. And then you go get a new dream based on the new reality. Why? Because if you don't live for a new dream, you end up living in the past! And there is no future in the past. You will never know the joy of what God can win in the future if you are consumed with lamenting what is lost in the past.

I did exactly what John suggested. I took a day, went out into the deep woods over an hour away, and held a funeral for all the plans I had for that season of life. I grieved for all the dreams that would never come true. I said things to God I have since begged Him to forgive. Then I went home, and spent the next few months getting a new dream. And the joy of being a dad to my fourth child, Jadon John, has proven to be an awesome gift. Sure, it was more demanding to start over, just as I feared. But I opened myself up to whatever new plans and dreams God had for me in this new reality of a family of four kids whose ages spanned more than fifteen years.

What plan or dream are you still holding on to in your life or career that God has long since asked you to put to rest? What options or opportunities that are no longer available to you have you not let go of? Maybe you need to hold a funeral, grieve, and move on to whatever God has next for you. You will never find the new dream unless you let go of the old one. Something old may have to die, but that may be the only way to allow something new to live.

If you're a leader, it's especially important for you to be honest with yourself about such things. Leaders can't lie to themselves and lead well. They can't afford to pretend. If you lead others, you need to look honestly at your plans and dreams. You need to be open to something new that God may be asking you to lead. Your people are depending on you for that.

John's Perspective

One of the hardest things I ever did was resign from my position as leader of Skyline Church. I loved the people there; it was a joy to be their pastor. But for the last several years that I was there, I knew I could not remain forever.

In 1976, I received a calling from God to have a ministry to leaders. In the late 1970s and early '80s, I saw that calling unfold as I worked first with pastors and then with business leaders around the country. In the early '90s, I was stretched very thin. Margaret kept telling me that I could not do both, but I didn't want to listen. I didn't want to leave the people of Skyline. And I had a dream of opening up a leadership center there where people from around the nation and the world could come to be trained in leadership.

In 1995, I finally accepted that it would be impossible to continue as I had, and I resigned from Skyline. I grieved that decision, but I've never regretted it. As a leader, I knew it was time. And making that decision opened other doors, including the founding of EQUIP, my non-profit organization that teaches leadership in 177 nations around the world.

Growth always requires hard decisions. Be prepared to make them. That's especially important if you are a leader. Leaders need to make the hard choices before others see them or are ready to make them. Then they need to help their people navigate the transition.

More than Just Performance

One of the great joys in life is seeing people who had been running the bases of life the wrong way turn around and live out God's game plan for the full life. Someone who fits that description well is my friend John Williams. John is a talented guy, a very good businessman.

When he graduated from college, he took a job as a manager trainee for Southeast Toyota Distributors, where he flourished. He was a guy who used his talent and worked hard every day. Up the career ladder he went until he achieved the position of executive vice president.

After working twenty years and reaching the top of his profession, John got restless and began looking for a new challenge. He decided to leave his secure corporate position in Florida and launch a Toyota dealership in the Northeast Metro Atlanta area. The business took off. Within two years it became the largest retail operation in the state and one of the top dealerships in the country. But as he progressively achieved great professional success, his personal life suffered some losses.

During the growth of his dealership, a colleague invited him to attend 12Stone. John had grown up in a good home and had gone to church as a kid, but as an adult, church wasn't a part of his life except for an Easter or Christmas service, or the occasional wedding. And truthfully, God wasn't really on his radar.

It didn't take long for the two of us to connect. We had a kindred entrepreneurial spirit. It was like iron sharpening iron. While I stirred his faith thinking, he stirred my business thinking. On Easter Sunday 2002, he accepted Christ. As God has challenged him to change and grow, he has accepted the challenge. "The one thing I have come to know," he says, "is when God calls on you, He expects obedience."

During the last ten years, while I've mentored John spiritually, he has mentored me in business, helping me understand more about finances and how business deals work. It's been a fantastic relationship.

John began to run the bases the right way. As he did, God began to do a deeper work and knit his heart with Jennifer, his new bride. John's love for his three kids from his earlier marriage increased as he sought to put God at the center of his life. His relationship with his ex-wife improved greatly. John and Jennifer's commitment to each other and running the bases according to God's design transformed the way they lived.

John has been on quite a journey. When he became part of the church, about a thousand people were attending every weekend. He put down roots. He started to give and serve. He began inviting friends, family, and business associates into the faith journey. When we were preparing to build a new building, he gave the first major check. And God continues to impress a passion for prayer upon his heart.

One day he and I sat down for a lunch at Olive Garden, and I shared the next part of the vision with him. God had birthed a dream for a leadership center that would be committed to serving present leaders and raising up the next-generation leaders. Furthermore, I told him that John Maxwell had agreed to lend his name for the center: It would be called the John Maxwell Leadership Center, and 12Stone would build it. It would become a home for EQUIP, John Maxwell's international non-profit leadership training organization. It would be the home base for 12Stone's residency program for next-generation ministry leaders. It would facilitate 12Stone's coaching of pastors and serving churches. It would hold John Maxwell's digital leadership library. And it would create a partnership with Wesley Seminary at Indiana Wesleyan University to train emerging church leaders.

My request to John Williams was this: "Would you help advise me in the process of approaching a donor for the leadership center? I have a guy in mind that I think will give the entire $5 million. I know it may sound crazy, but I think God will provide."

John Williams is a gifted visionary and very smart businessman. For nearly a year, he was my confidant in this hope to raise the $5 million. Unfortunately, it never came to be. So we found ourselves at a dead end. Sitting at another Olive Garden lunch, we discussed it, and John suddenly asked, "What if I was the guy God wanted to use to give the $5 million?" I was in shock. It had never crossed my mind. It was just too much money.

What I didn't know was that God was moving in John in ways that would be hard to explain. In short, he sensed that God might be opening a door for him to sell his Atlanta businesses. If God did that, then he would make the $5 million donation.

As only God works, it actually happened just as John Williams had envisioned.

We all celebrated as John Williams's life intersected with John Maxwell's for the sake of raising leaders that will change future generations. Only God can take a third-base runner like John Williams who was bent on performance and make his impact so much more than performance. He has made the move from marketplace success to kingdom significance. That is the final step in running the bases in life—scoring. And we'll discuss that more in the final chapter.

John's Growth Guide

Discussion Questions

1. Do you agree that God has woven a desire and an expectation for growth into the fabric of the world? What evidence do you see for or against that idea? Explain.

2. How well are you handling the pace of progress in your career? Do you find it to be rewardingly fast, frustratingly slow, or somewhere in between? Have you always reacted to the pace as you do now?

3. What do you do to help yourself develop appropriate patience, cultivate a willingness to serve your boss and organization, and earn your keep every day?

4. Describe a failure you experienced at work, in your career, or in an area of high interest that you handled well. What was the key to your ability to do well in that situation? Is that how you typically handle difficulties? Explain. How can you apply that key to other areas of your life?

(Continued)

5. How do you see your natural talent? Are you satisfied with what you have? Or do you wish you had more talent or a different talent? How has this impacted the way you approach your career? Has it helped or hindered you? How could you change your attitude to help you become more successful?

6. Is your natural inclination to spend too much time and effort on your work and career or too little? How has that inclination created problems or challenges for you? What would you consider to be a healthy approach to work and career? What are you willing to do to try to achieve it in your life?

Assignment

For many years I have admonished people to avoid having destination disease. How? By allowing God to change your plans and always being willing to give up your sling for a sword. To put yourself in the best place to keep learning and growing, take some time to do the following:

A. **Perform a Funeral:** You may be like Kevin and need to put to rest a dream that is not in alignment with God's plan for your life. Your out-of-date dream may be due to a change in season for your life. Or it may be necessary to give up a dream because the talent you have doesn't match up with it. Or maybe God has something else for you that would honor and glorify Him more. If any of these apply to you, set a time and place to have a private funeral for that outdated dream. You may even want to symbolically bury some object that represents the dream. Grieve. Pour your heart out to God. Then open your mind and heart to whatever God has next for you.

B. **Pick Up a Sword:** Is God inviting you to new challenges and opportunities in your life and career? If He is, you will not be able to accomplish them with the same tools that got you to where you are today. Like David, you must be willing to put down your sling and take up your sword.

What does that represent to you in your career? First, identify your sling. What skill have you used up to now to be successful? Try to determine how your reliance on it now could be holding you back. Then try to discern what new skill would take you farther on to the next level. Once you've identified it, create a concrete plan to acquire it. Be sure to include the time and resources that will be needed along with specific deadlines.

9

Scoring: How to Keep Living and Winning God's Way

When you play baseball, getting to third base is exciting. But it's not scoring. In fact, if you always got stranded at third base and never made it home, you'd find it frustrating and disappointing. A run doesn't get added to the scoreboard until you cross home plate. And that's the whole point when it comes to baseball. In order to win, you have to score.

In life's spiritual journey, many people get stranded on third base. Truly, work matters. So do business results and economic success. But ultimately, these things are not a worthy end in themselves. To be successful, we need to get back to home plate. There's no home run without that—in baseball or in life. The bottom line is that you will not be satisfied with your life every day, every week, every year, and over your lifetime unless you complete the diamond and fulfill the purpose for which God put you on this earth. That's the only way to score in God's game plan for life.

Will You Make Up Your Mind?

Why don't more people succeed according to God's plan? Why do they get stuck on third base? I believe one of the main reasons is that people are confused about who they are going to serve. The Bible calls this double-mindedness. The book of James says that many of our prayers for material wants and for life's desires go unfulfilled because we want God to serve us instead of wanting to serve God.[1] We say we trust God and want His will for our lives, but we give in to our own selfish interests instead. Even the early disciples did this. Remember that James and John wanted to sit on the right and left of Jesus once He established His kingdom. They were supposed to be serving Jesus and their fellow human beings, but somehow they made it about serving themselves.

That's a danger for all of us. How are you doing in this area? Do you exist to serve God or do you think God exists to serve you? If you haven't settled this, you will be double-minded, vacillating back and forth between these two ways of thinking. As a result, you will never really get anywhere in life.

Let me show how this can impact you by giving you an example. I live in the northeast suburbs of Atlanta, Georgia. Imagine that I have a week of vacation over the Christmas break and I'm trying to make up my mind about where my family and I should go. We could go to my hometown of Grand Rapids, Michigan. That has a lot of appeal. It's where I grew up. It's where I first served as a pastor. I have family and lots of friends there. I think we would have a blast, so on the first day of vacation, we set off on the eight-hundred-mile drive.

We travel five hundred miles that first day. When we stop at the hotel for the night, it's cold. And that's when I start to think about what it's like in Michigan in December. The average temperature is twenty-seven degrees. There's ice and snow everywhere. That's not very appealing. The next morning when we get up, it's freezing. And that's when I realize, it's going to be a long time until summer's warmth. Why are we headed north?

"Okay, everybody," I say to the family, "change of plan. We're headed to Key West!" We turn the car south and start driving. We're all thinking about seventy-five-degree weather and tropical breezes. We drive south and pass back through Atlanta. On the second day, we stop in northern Florida. Fantastic. In one more day of driving, we'll be in Key West.

But then I have second thoughts. I told my family and friends in Michigan that we would see them. To just bail on them isn't right. And so we head north again. We drive for two more days. But then we hit the cold again, and I'm reminded about how much I hate the snow and ice. I start dreaming about warm weather again. We stay in the hotel an extra day to decide, and then it hits me. We've used up six of our seven days. The only thing we can do now is use the last day to drive back home.

The Bible says that double-minded people are unstable in all their ways. Like me when I can't decide on how to spend my vacation, they never arrive anywhere worthwhile.

John's Perspective

One of my favorite real-life stories about decision-making involves Ronald Reagan when he was a boy. His aunt offered to have a pair of shoes made for him. When the shoemaker measured his feet, he asked the boy whether he wanted the shoes to have round toes or square toes. The boy couldn't decide. A few days later the shoemaker saw the boy on the street and asked what he had decided about the shoes.

"I haven't made up my mind yet," he answered.

"Very well," said the shoemaker. "Your shoes will be ready tomorrow."

> When Reagan picked up the shoes, one had a round toe and the other a square toe. It was a lesson in decision making that the future president never forgot.

Perhaps *doubleminded* or *indecisive* describes the faith journey for the majority of the people in our country who call themselves Christians. They never really get anywhere because they won't make up their mind about whom they're going to serve. For a few days or weeks or months, they say, "I'm here to serve God." For some length of time, they travel in God's direction. They worship God every seven days. They spend time daily reading the Bible and praying. They seek God's wisdom, obey His prompts, and serve others.

But then they get distracted. They drift into their old habits. They skip church. They fail to tithe. They forget to read the Bible. They stop praying most of the time. When they do remember to talk to God, it's a give-me prayer: *God, please give me a good day, give me the raise I've been hoping for, give me that thing I've been wanting.* They get absorbed in the pressures of life and hope that God will serve them as they travel down the road of life on their own agenda. Even if they know the value of God's game plan, they're back to running the bases of life the wrong way.

The good news is that we can change. We don't have to run life's bases the world's way. We can accept God's invitation to run opposite the world's pattern, as described in Romans 12:1–2. I've discussed verse 2 a lot in *Home Run*, but the key to winning this battle is contained in verse 1: *"I urge you, brothers and sisters, in view of God's mercy, to offer your bodies as a living sacrifice, holy and pleasing to God—this is your true and proper worship.* Do not conform to the pattern of this world, but be transformed by the renewing of your mind. Then you will be able to test and approve what God's will is— his good, pleasing and perfect will"* (emphasis added).

What an interesting picture: a living sacrifice. What is the essential characteristic of all sacrifices? They die! To conform to God's pattern, you must die to self—your selfish desires and sinful patterns of life—and in so dying, you actually live for God. Isn't it curious that our living death produces life to the full? To get the more in life that we desire—the more that God has put in us and wants to give us—we must give more to God. We must give our whole heart and life.

Glory Days

Our culture encourages us to chase personal glory. Many people are impressed by it. For example, you see it in sports all the time. We are amazed by athletes who can make spectacular dunks on the basketball court. *Wow!* we say, *can you believe he just did that?* Why are we so impressed? Because mere human beings created the game! We set the height of the rim at ten feet off the ground, clearly within reach of many people—not me, but many. But what if we had set the rim height at thirty feet? No basketball player would get any glory. As human beings, we put things within our reach and then we celebrate our accomplishments.

The same thing happens in baseball. The distance from home plate to the wall in most stadiums is around 325 feet at the foul line and 400 or so feet in center field. If a baseball player can hit seven hundred home runs in a career, he's enshrined in the hall of fame in Cooperstown. But what if the home run fence was set at, say, a mile, or ten miles, or a thousand miles? No glory. Isaiah 66:1 says that the earth is God's footstool. I think God could dunk a basketball no matter how high it is, because He'd have to bend down to reach it. And He could hit a baseball to Jupiter if He wanted to.

We give *glory* to people too cheaply. We are impressed with way too little. We say humankind can accomplish amazing things, but that's only compared with other humans. It's all small potatoes compared with God. So if you're going to give your praise and glory to someone, raise the bar for what impresses you and give glory to the only one deserving it: God!

You cannot have a home run life by making the pursuit of personal glory your goal. Significance in life does not come from glorifying yourself. It comes from giving God greater glory. We can't divide our hearts and minds and expect to succeed according to God's game plan. We need to center our lives on God and give Him all the glory.

King Solomon of ancient Israel, said to be the wisest man who ever lived, figured this out nearly three thousand years ago. In the book of Ecclesiastes, Solomon recounts how he lived in accordance with the world's standards, trying everything that human beings promise will bring fulfillment: work, wealth, projects, hobbies, sex, success. He says he withheld from himself no pleasure. But all these things were meaningless. He calls them "a chasing after the wind."[2] A life of selfish pursuit without limits brought Solomon to one conclusion:

> There's no end to the publishing of books, and constant study wears you out so you're no good for anything else. The last and final word is this:
>
> *Fear God.*
> *Do what he tells you.*
>
> And that's it. Eventually God will bring everything that we do out into the open and judge it according to its hidden intent, whether it's good or evil.[3]

In other words, the best possible life comes from revering God and obeying Him. That's how we score in life according to God's plan.

We would be wise to realize that this is God's way of trying to help us right-size what is truly significant in life, what matters from an eternal perspective. If we don't *right-size* our thinking, we will do what our culture does: wrong-size what is significant in life. We live in a culture that tends to supersize earthly things and downsize eternal things.

John's Perspective

When I was a boy, my father took me to hear the great preacher E. Stanley Jones speak. After the message, I went with my dad to meet Dr. Jones, who laid his hands on me and prayed for me. It was an incredible experience.

Dr. Jones once said that anything less than God will let you down. Why? Because anything less than God is not rooted in eternity!

If we don't realize the importance of the spiritual world and try to get outside of ourselves and attempt to embrace eternity, we become very shortsighted. We become like children when they are about to enter high school. What do I mean by that? Going to school seems to take forever when you're growing up. And after all the years in elementary school and then middle school, when you arrive at high school it seems very important. You think it's the culmination. In fact, you may believe that high school is real life. You can end up living for those high school moments instead of living for your future.

Caring parents try to help their kids avoid this trap. "Listen," they say, "high school is *preparation* for real life; it's not real life. Those four years lead to maybe four years of college and then to forty years of doing real life. Don't get consumed with high school and make foolish decisions because you thought it was real life."

I had these repeated conversations with my daughter, Julisa. Like most girls, she sometimes felt that high school acceptance or rejection and the drama of relationships was defining her life. I used to tell her,

"Sure, it matters to you today. But don't live for it like it's the end of life. High school will pass. The memories of winners and losers in sports and popularity will fade as fast as graduation. Before long, you'll move from being the top of the high school senior class to the bottom rung of being freshmen in college. You'll rise in college only to graduate and enter the work world at the bottom again. The real-life pressures of getting a job, being responsible for yourself, getting married to the guy you choose to love will one day make you look back and laugh at how seriously you took high school." And that's what's happened. Julisa is done with college, has gotten her first teaching job, and has gotten married. Her life looks so much bigger now than high school.

We need to realize that life on earth is high school. While we're in it, it looks like everything. But compared with eternity and God's glory, it's small. I believe eternity will reveal that our life here was only preparation. So are you living for high school, meaning your time on earth? Because when you live for life on earth, you tend to fear people instead of God. And then you tend to do what this world tells you to do instead of what God tells you. Are you seeing the bigger picture and serving God for the sake of eternity? Or are you scrapping for your own temporary glory?

Jesus tried to get this message across in so many ways, saying:

- "Watch out! Be on your guard against all kinds of greed; life does not consist in an abundance of possessions."[4]
- "Do not store up for yourselves treasures on earth, where moths and vermin destroy, and where thieves break in and steal. But store up for yourselves treasures in heaven, where moths and vermin do not destroy, and where thieves do not break in and steal. For where your treasure is, there your heart will be also."[5]
- "What good will it be for someone to gain the whole world, yet forfeit their soul? Or what can anyone give in exchange for their soul?"[6]

Despite what the bumper sticker says, the one who dies with the most toys does not win. As Peter the Apostle said, everything in this material world is going to burn up—houses, trophies, cars, jewelry, money, technology, art, transportation, monuments, cities.[7] It will be the ultimate bonfire. Knowing that, how should we live our lives? We should exist for God and His glory.

The Apostle Paul understood this. It was a recurring theme in his letters. He wrote,

- "God exalted him [Jesus] to the highest place and gave him the name that is above every name, that at the name of Jesus every knee should bow, in heaven and on earth and under the earth, and every tongue acknowledge that Jesus Christ is Lord, to the *glory* of God the Father" (emphasis added).[8]
- "For from him and through him and for him are all things. To him be the *glory* forever! Amen" (emphasis added).[9]
- "So whether you eat or drink or whatever you do, do it all for the *glory* of God" (emphasis added).[10]

Is it any wonder that the first question and answer in the Westminster Larger Catechism are as follows:

Question: What is the chief and highest end of man?

Answer: To glorify God, and fully to enjoy Him forever.

That was written in the 1640s. If we were writing it today, perhaps it would say to glorify God and serve Him forever.

Life is so uncertain; God is not. We have no control over many of the circumstances or outcomes of our lives. Life is often demanding, difficult, and painful. And we face seasons and cycles of uncertainty. We work hard, but then an economic downturn flips our lives upside down. We strive to stay healthy but cancer shows up on the scene anyway. We spend decades planning for retirement, but a heart attack takes us out before we can enjoy it. We pray for miracles that do not come. We dream of having a child, yet it never comes despite all of medicine's advances. Or we're blessed with children, only to see them choose a wayward and destructive life.

If the only thing you live for on earth is yourself, you will be disappointed. No wonder people dive deeper into debt, give in to every indulgence, become addicted, escape into substance abuse, or contemplate suicide. God invites us to live larger. He wants us to know that we are made for Him and for eternity. We have a purpose greater than earth. We have been bought with a price, with the blood of Jesus Christ, and we have a future with Him that we are preparing for on earth. We can choose to live in a way that brings God glory. And that glory will last! It never fades.

How to Score by Giving God Glory

Of all the things God shares—the breath of life, His son Jesus, His blessings and favor—His glory is not on the list. In fact, He cannot share His glory. Why? Because He cannot lie. We are the created, not the Creator. Nothing done by our hand compares to what God does. If we want a home run life, we need to bring our talents, skills, and whatever third-base success God entrusts to us back to God at home plate. In that way, we can make our lives count for something bigger than ourselves or our brief time on earth. How do we do that? By doing these four things:

1. Do What You Were Created to Do...For God's Glory

Whenever the purpose of something God has created is fulfilled, God is glorified. Study nature and you sense the truth of this. When you see a flower bloom, there is a beauty to it, not just visually, but in the fact that the plant is doing what it was made to do. When you see an eagle soar on the wind, it brings glory to God as it fulfills its created purpose.

In contrast, when something is misused for a purpose contrary to its created nature, God is not glorified. This is easy to see when the things people create are used for a wrong purpose. You could probably drive a nail into a piece of wood using a wrench or a book or a heavy vase, but a hammer works much better. And it is unlikely to get damaged in the process. This is one of the reasons sin doesn't glorify God. Sin damages you, hurts others, and wastes your life. When we violate something's created purpose, it distorts the value and purpose of the created thing. Sin always has a cost and creates the need to clean up a mess.

There is a pleasure and beauty that comes from something or someone fulfilling purpose. You can even see it in the way people run the bases of life God's way. When a person prays to God at home plate and feels a sense of peace, God is glorified. When someone does the hard thing at first base by telling the truth instead of taking an easy way out, God is glorified. When a mother cares for her infant or an adult child serves an elderly parent, these actions at second base glorify God. And at third base, when a teacher helps a student to finally understand, or a talented singer stands onstage and communicates a song, or an entrepreneur raises a company from nothing and uses it to serve customers, God is glorified.

People know when something or someone is fulfilling purpose. When you witness it, something inside you resonates. When it happens, there is undeniable beauty. Non-believers sense it, but often don't know what to attribute it to. Believers know to give God the glory. Psalm 29:1–2 describes it well:

> *Ascribe to the LORD, you heavenly beings,*
> *ascribe to the LORD glory and strength.*

Ascribe to the LORD the glory due his name;
worship the LORD in the splendor of his holiness.

When we do the things God created us to do, and we ascribe to Him the glory, we point out the greatness of God to the world. But we must do it in the right spirit. That's key. The Apostle Paul confirmed this in his letters to the church. When speaking to slaves, he advised, "Whatever you do, work at it with all your heart, as working for the Lord, not for human masters, since you know that you will receive an inheritance from the Lord as a reward. It is the Lord Christ you are serving."[11] It's possible to glorify God in the smallest of actions—even in the way we eat and drink. Paul admonished, "Whatever you do, do it all for the glory of God."[12]

If your motivation is to serve for God's glory instead of your own, every act that uses your gifts becomes an act of worship, a glorification of God. When you cook dinner. When you serve a friend. When you earn a dollar. When you do your work. When you help a child. If your heart is for God, so will be your actions.

2. Give Yourself Away...For God's Glory

When Joseph dreamed about himself standing while others were bowing, he thought it was a vision of his future glory. By the time the dream was actually fulfilled, Joseph understood that it was really about serving others for God's glory. Remember, when his brothers threw themselves down at his feet in Egypt, Joseph said, "Don't be afraid. Am I in the place of God? You intended to harm me, but God intended it for good to accomplish what is now being done, the saving of many lives. So then, don't be afraid. I will provide for you and your children." The passage goes on to say that he reassured them and spoke kindly to them.[13]

As a boy of seventeen, Joseph thought the dream was about

third-base success. But it was really about the power and purpose that comes from going all the way around the bases in the right direction and returning to God at home plate. It was never about Joseph's success. It was about Joseph's serving, about spending his life for something greater than himself.

God always has something greater than our mere success in mind when He leads us in the journey of life. Most often His greater purpose for us relates to saving people, as it did for Joseph. It's about serving and reaching others in Jesus's name. Jesus admonished His disciples that whatever power they had was to be used to help others. He redefined greatness, saying, "Whoever wants to become great among you must be your servant, and whoever wants to be first must be your slave—just as the Son of Man did not come to be served, but to serve, and to give his life as a ransom for many."[14]

John's Perspective

In 2012, my non-profit organization EQUIP hosted a leadership conference in South Florida for the volunteer leaders from 177 nations who have worked to train leaders all around the world. I was very excited about it because it would be the first time in EQUIP's sixteen-year history that these leaders and many of the American volunteers and donors would gather together.

We held many training sessions, hosted informative meetings, and enjoyed times of worship led by Darlene Zschech, but none of those were the highlight of the event. For me, the greatest moment was when EQUIP's leaders washed the feet of the international representatives who had been leading and serving around the world. It was our opportunity to express our gratitude to them in the most symbolic way we could. It was one of the most significant nights of my life.

At 12Stone Church we express this idea as "giving ourselves away," and it is one of our core beliefs. It's the nature of God to give—"For God so loved the world that he gave his one and only son"[15]—so we desire to emulate God's example. At 12Stone, which we think of as our post, we believe God has asked us to give ourselves away in order to reach the lost, serve the least, and raise up leaders. We believe that is how we become the hand and heart of God to the world around us.

I remember the day that God began to impress on my heart the value of giving ourselves away. The church was sixteen years old, and I knew that our next move was to become a multi-campus church, to be one church with many locations. I began searching for our next location, and when I came across a grocery store that had closed, I was convinced I had found it. I began the regular practice of stopping by the property and praying for God to use that place to change lives for His glory.

Some months went by, and I felt it was time to make a leadership move. I was preparing to cast vision and raise funds when I discovered a temporary sign at the building indicating that another church was going to make it their home.

I was ticked. "What a waste of time," I complained to God. "I've spent a lot of time praying. Now it's been taken. I don't even get that, Lord. That would've been a great place for a church."

"It *is* a great place for a church," I sensed God communicating to me, "and it *is* a church. The only problem seems to be that it's not *yours*!"

"You know what I mean, Lord," I responded, knowing I was now in an argument I could not win. "I wanted that for your glory."

"It will be."

"Okay—fine. It's for your glory."

"Son," I felt God saying, "if you were going to raise funds for it when you thought it would be yours to lead, then still raise funds for it. Give yourself away."

In that moment, I felt like I was Jacob wrestling with God. *I can't raise money for another church*, I thought. *That will mess up what I'm doing at my church.* It seemed foolish. God asked me to lead 12Stone. *What if our people give to this church and we get less? What if we become less?* I thought.

I could not deny that God wanted me to do this. So I talked to my board. They thought it was a good idea. Now I couldn't escape it. So I shared the whole story with 12Stone and confessed my restlessness. Then I invited them to give themselves away so another church could win. And with no prior notice, just responding in the moment, they gave generously! I was still uncomfortable. Nonetheless, I added my personal check and felt like God was honored by our obedience.

At the end of that Sunday, Marcia asked, "How much did we personally give?" When I told her, she said, "Well, I have to tell you, God gave me a number that was ten times that amount."

"Wow, really!" I answered. "'Cause He didn't tell me that."

"Well, He told me!" she responded.

I sighed.

"Okay, you and God win." And we wrote another personal check for ten times our first. Marcia smiled. I think God smiled as well.

That week I called up the pastor, whom I'd never met, and he agreed to meet me at Starbucks, still unaware of the purpose of the meeting. Then I told him the story, handing him the check from our church that was in the neighborhood of $35,000, which was big for us. I know it blew him away, but curiously it also changed me. And it changed our church. God was reminding us that it's not about us and our glory. It's about giving ourselves away for His glory.

Since then as a church, we've given away the first 10 percent of what we receive in general offerings. Candidly, God often asks us to give far more as we continue to learn how to give ourselves away. We hope that it is an expression of what Jesus challenged His disciples to do in Matthew 5:16 when He said, "Let your light shine before others, that they may see your good deeds and glorify your Father in heaven."

I don't know why it seems so hard to learn this lesson. But I was marked by the words of novelist Stephen King. In his commencement speech to Vassar College in May 2001, he talked about the importance of people giving themselves away. He said,

> That human life is brief when placed in time's wider perspective is something we all know. I am asking you to consider it on a more visceral level, that's all … What will you do? Well, I'll tell you one thing you're not going to do, and that's take it with you …
>
> We come in naked and broke. We may be dressed when we go out, but we're just as broke. Warren Buffett? Going to go out broke. Bill Gates? Going to go out broke. Tom Hanks? Going out broke … Steve King? Broke. You guys? Broke … And how long in between? … Just the blink of an eye …
>
> Yet for a short period—let's say forty years, but the merest blink in the larger course of things—you and your contemporaries will wield enormous power … .That's your time, your moment. Don't miss it. I think my generation did, although I don't blame us too much; it's over in the blink of an eye and it's easy to miss …
>
> Should you give away what you have? Of course you should. I want you to consider making your lives one long gift to others, and why not? All you have is on loan, anyway … All that lasts is what you pass on. The rest is smoke and mirrors …
>
> Giving isn't about the receiver or the gift but the giver. It's for the giver. One doesn't open one's wallet to improve the world, although it's nice when that happens; one does it to improve one's self … Giving is a way of taking the focus off

the money we make and putting it back where it belongs—on the lives we lead, the families we raise, the communities which nurture us...

So I ask you to begin the next great phase of your life by giving, and to continue as you begin. I think you'll find in the end that you got far more than you ever had, and did more good than you ever dreamed.[16]

I don't know anything about Stephen King's faith. Maybe he's a believer; maybe he's not. But either way, he understands that we are here on earth not merely to gain for ourselves but to give ourselves away. As Christ followers, we know we do so for God's glory.

At 12Stone, we're inspired by the story of the Good Samaritan and offer our people a motto: "Get off your donkey." We challenge them to do something for someone who is beat up on the road of life. That's what separated the Good Samaritan from everyone else. Mere good intentions as you walk by people in need are meaningless. We need to get off our donkeys and help. That gives God glory!

3. Invite Others into the Faith Journey...For God's Glory

Nothing we can do while on this earth is more important than leading another person to find and follow Christ. While we can see the value of being God's hands and showing His heart to others, we can never forget that God did not send Jesus to give His life for the saving of physical life. He did so for giving *eternal* life. Everything on earth will burn up in the great fire at the end of the world, but the soul of every person will last forever. Paul writes in 2 Corinthians 5:16–20 that we have been entrusted with the ministry of reconciliation. Our job is to invite people into the spiritual journey and show them the way to Christ if they will let us.

Sometimes people come to us and we tell them about Christ. That was the case with Chris Huff. The church had been open for only a couple of years when Chris showed up with his wife, Lisa, and their three young children.

"I came to appease my wife," Chris was very quick to tell me. "I just want you to know that I don't believe in any of this stuff."

Chris called himself an atheist. "Well then," I responded, "would you like to shut down a church?"

"I would!" Chris responded with enthusiasm.

"Then meet with me over a few lunches and convince me that the Bible is a hoax," I challenged. "If you can, I'll close the church. If not, join Jesus and the church. What do you say?"

Today Chris is on staff. He went from skeptic, to believer, to follower of Christ, to lay minister, to full-time vocational pastor.

Chris came to me because I'm a pastor. But the ministry of reconciliation isn't supposed to be confined within the walls of the church. I try to invite people into the spiritual journey everywhere I encounter them: in my neighborhood, at the gym, during my kids' activities. So should you.

Wherever God has you on the map, God has you on mission. The people around you in every area of life—at work, in the park, in your neighborhood or community, on the golf course—are there for you to invite into the faith journey. Maybe you should invite someone to your church where they will hear the truth over time. Maybe you should be a sounding board for someone who is trying to navigate through life's difficulties. Perhaps God wants you to be more direct and share your faith story. Keep your eyes and ears open. God makes His appeal through us. We need to be mindful of the opportunities God gives us and be sensitive to the promptings of the Holy Spirit.

As followers of Christ, we don't ever have the option to quit caring about others. Most of the people in the world around us do not know Jesus. I was reminded of this several years ago during a season when I was worn out. I had grown weary from the effort of adding more services, the work of expanding buildings, and the grind of teaching something God-centered and culturally current every seven days.

"How long do I have to keep pushing to reach more and more people?" I muttered to God during one of my prayer times.

He seemed interested in using this for a conversation. "You have three kids"—which I did at that time. Then came the next thought. "Well, son, here's what I want you to do. First, write all three names in your journal." I did. "Now," God continued, "circle two names. Those two will spend eternity with me. The other one will not! You pick."

I cannot describe to you the emotional turmoil that erupted in my soul. Somehow, I was able to internalize the intensity of that moment. I literally began to weep. The thought of one of my children spending eternity without God undid me. I was shattered as through tears I pleaded, "Never, God. You have made yourself too real for me to deny. So I cannot bear the thought of my children being separated from you. If you give me three kids, then you take all three to heaven."

In the intensity of that moment, the Holy Spirit then softly spoke, "When two out of three is okay for you, it's okay for me. Until then, reach people like they are your kids."

That right-sized my thinking. We are always in danger of making the church about us, making it about the people already in the church instead of about those who are not yet there. We need to give our lives to what really matters, to what lasts. We cannot have a home run life if we are not attending to the eternal life of other people. Giving ourselves away to reach spiritually lost people not only changes people's lives, it also glorifies God.

4. Help Others Discover What They Were Created to Do...For God's Glory

I believe all people have a purpose, given to them by God. Ephesians 2:10 says, "We are God's handiwork, created in Christ Jesus to do good works, which God prepared in advance for us to do," so it's pretty clear that there are things God wants us to do in this world. However, not all of us are able to figure out on our own what God created us to do. Some people need help figuring that out. That is also part of what we are here on earth to do, because it also glorifies God when you help others discover their gifts and use them to fulfill God's purpose for their lives.

That process starts by helping people to grow in faith—by winning with God and winning within. It continues by helping them learn to win with others. And it grows as we help them to win results and complete the circuit of the diamond at home plate, doing what God created them to do.

I have been the recipient of much help in the area of finding and pursuing my purpose, not the least of which has come from John Maxwell. His mentoring has been unexplainably kind and generous. It has been at the core of this home run journey for me. John's stated desire to add value to others is not a cliché or idle words for him. It's a conviction and a calling.

Because I've learned so much from John and it has been so valuable to me in my life and career, it's been my desire to pass it on to other leaders. That soon became a central part of the calling of 12Stone Church, too. The question became how to do it. As a church, we knew we wanted to take responsibility for raising up another generation of leaders, but how?

It soon became clear to me that we needed to create a leadership center. It would be a place where young ministry leaders could learn from the leadership teachings of John and others and then practice the skills they learned by doing ministry in the local church. We would create a residency that would bring in college graduates and invest in their ministry leadership development. They would learn in a way similar to how young doctors learn to practice medicine in hospitals during their residencies.

As this idea became clearer to me, the church board, and the staff, God put it in my heart to talk to John about naming it the John Maxwell Leadership Center. My first desire was to honor John for a lifetime of adding value to kingdom leaders. My second desire was to draw from John's leadership principles and deliver them afresh into the world of next-generation leaders. As you already know, John agreed to this, and we are ecstatic. These efforts to help others discover and develop in the things God created them to do will be part of John's ongoing legacy.

John's Perspective

I explained in the previous chapter that when I was leading Skyline Church, it was my dream to create a leadership center. It was one of my greatest desires. I believe that everything rises and falls on leadership, and that the way to make the greatest impact on the world is to develop leaders. It's why I founded EQUIP. It's why I've dedicated nearly forty years to training leaders.

When I gave up leading Skyline, I knew I was laying down the dream of creating the leadership center. That was very painful to me. So I cannot adequately explain what it meant to me the day Kevin approached me to say 12Stone would be founding a leadership center and asked whether they could name it after me. I was dumbfounded—and so very grateful to God. The Lord was doing for me something I could not do for myself. He was doing it better than I could have done it. And I was not being asked to do a single thing to bring it about other than to give it my blessing. What a gift!

This is just the way God is. You cannot out-give Him. When God asked me to mentor Kevin, I gladly did it. I believe in investing in leaders, and Kevin was a talented kid. But I never expected anything from it. Here's what's happened, though: I've gotten back from Kevin way more than I've given him. The return has been fantastic. But Kevin and I both know it's not because of him or me. It's all because of God. And it is our desire that He receive all the glory.

Completing the Bases

When Jesus taught us to stockpile treasures in heaven, He was challenging us to have a home run view of life. He was reminding us that our true home is in heaven for eternity, and that we should live our lives as if we know it. One man who did that was Doug Edwards.

I first met Doug when 12Stone was looking for land in the late 1990s. We were quickly outgrowing the 250 seats in the first facility we had built. We were in multiple services, and knew it wouldn't be long before we would need to find more property and expand. Soon after I started looking around, I discovered there was a fourteen-acre plot of land on a major highway about a mile from the church building we were in. It was obviously someone's homestead, but I recognized that it would be a fantastic location for a church.

We had no money to buy it, but one day, I drove up to the homestead determined to meet the owner and begin a conversation. I wasn't sure what to say, and by time I got to the door I'd lost my courage. I literally turned around, got in my car, and drove away. *What a wimp!* I thought. "God," I pleaded, "I don't know what to do. Help me."

Sometimes the hand of God just has to take over.

Weeks later on a sunny afternoon, a friend asked me to join him on the golf course. I met him there, and he had a business investor with him by the name of Doug Edwards. To my utter shock, I learned that Doug lived on the fourteen-acre homestead I had found. It had been in his family for over thirty years. What more could a pastor ask for? God had arranged an introduction.

It took me a long time to summon the courage to talk to Doug about the property, but finally I asked him to breakfast. I bought him a doughnut and said, "Doug, your land would be a great place for a church."

He was kind, but it was like he was patting my head and humoring me. He said, "Son, you can't afford it!"

"I didn't say I wanted to pay for it," I quickly retorted. He laughed and that was the end of it.

Doug was right. We could not afford it. The land's value was about $1 million. But when you believe God has a bigger dream than the one you're living, you deepen your dependence and learn to pray with greater intensity.

A few months later, I asked Doug if I could walk on his property from time to time. He agreed, which was a mistake for Doug. Because I was walking the land and praying Deuteronomy 11:24 over it, which says, "Every place where you set your foot will be yours." I prayed and walked the land every week, asking for God to put it in Doug's heart to invest in the kingdom of God by giving the land to the church. Yeah, it sounds ridiculous, since Doug did not even attend our church. But we served the same God, and we needed a miracle.

Months later over another morning doughnut, Doug said he'd been praying and felt like the land would be a great place for a church. He said he'd landed on a price and would be happy to meet with the board and explain the offer.

I was both eager and apprehensive about this news. When I met with the board of elders to tell them about Doug's offer, I also explained what I really believed: "Doug is coming to the next meeting, and I believe God's told him to just give us the land. This will change our church and change people's lives."

One of my board members laughed and said, "Does anyone want what the pastor's been smoking?"

Let's just say they didn't share my belief. But they did agree for us to meet with Doug. Meanwhile, I kept praying.

When the day of the meeting arrived, I sat across the table from Doug. I was ready to sign papers for the purchase. But Doug looked at me and said, "I believe God wants me to give this land for you to build a church." He signed the property over to us on the spot. My board couldn't believe it. And all I could say was, "Now does anybody want what the pastor is smoking?" That was a defining moment for all of us.

Doug Edwards was very successful in business. But what he modeled that day was how to leverage earthly success for eternal significance. Doug used mere money to make a kingdom impact. It was a home run decision to change people's lives for God and for good.

Doug went to be with the Lord before we could construct the new worship center. But since then, God has allowed 12Stone to lead several thousand people to faith in Christ. I consider every soul we reach, every person beat up on the road of life that we serve, every leader we raise up to be a bit more treasure stored up in heaven for Doug.

That's our calling—to be a force for God and for good. We are to point people to God, give Him glory, and give ourselves away in the process. What does that mean in a practical sense? It means to live life according to God's game plan: Love God (home plate), love yourself (first base), love others (second base), love what you do (third base), and do all for the glory of God (score). That kind of home run life gives itself away, and gets more back than it ever dreamed!

John's Application Guide

Discussion Questions

1. Is it possible for someone who runs the bases the right way to still get stuck at third base and not make it back to home plate by failing to fulfill a greater purpose for God? Explain.
2. Whose glory are you living for? Have you made a definitive commitment to serve God in your life? Or are you still on the fence? What, if anything, is holding you back?

(Continued)

3. If you have decided to live for God's glory, how do you hold yourself accountable for keeping your efforts focused in that direction instead of drifting away and seeking your own glory?

4. What kinds of things help you to have and keep an eternal perspective? Do you have regular practices to help you with this? If not, what are you willing to do to develop and maintain some?

5. A greater sense of purpose that uses our talents for God's glory unfolds slowly for most people. In addition, how much God reveals of that purpose is often related to people's season of life:

- Foundation: Core preparation for the future.
- Self-Discovery: Learning who you are and what you can do.
- Skill Development: Gaining experience and honing skills.
- Execution: Intentionally using your skills and talents for kingdom work.
- Investing: Entrusting the next generation with your skills and resources.

(Note: Seasons often overlap.)

Based on these ideas, which season do you believe you're in? What do you do to remain content with the season?

6. What do you believe you were created to do? If you're not sure, what steps can you take to figure it out? If you do have a strong sense of purpose, how can you use it to give greater glory to God?

Assignment

Set aside time to explore ways in which you can live for a greater purpose than just yourself:

A. **Give Yourself Away:** What skills, talents, resources, and opportunities do you have that you can put at God's disposal for His glory and greater purpose? Pray and make a list. Then seek insight from God on how to proceed. The answers you find may be for a season or for the rest of your life. Remain open-minded to what God prompts.

B. **Help Others in the Faith Journey:** Who has God put into your life? Chances are, He has put them there for a reason. Which people are spiritually unresolved? Make a list. Pray for them. Engage with them. Look for opportunities to talk about faith issues. Be sensitive to their challenges and struggles. There may be opportunities to help them understand that God loves them and wants to help them.

What about the believers in your life? Many may need your help strengthening their faith, finding their purpose, or using their gifts. Make yourself available to give yourself away to them for God's greater glory.

Notes

Chapter 1 The Life You Want: Introduction by John C. Maxwell

1. John W. Kennedy, "The Debt Slayers," *Christianity Today*, 1 May 2006, http://www.christianitytoday.com/ct/2006/may/23.40.html, accessed 11 November 2010.
2. "Statistics and Information on Pornography in the USA," BlazingGrace .org, http://www.blazinggrace.org/cms/bg/pornstats, accessed 11 November 2010.
3. "New Marriage and Divorce Statistics Released," 31 March 2008, http://www.barna.org/family-kids-articles/42-new-marriage-and-divorce-statistics-released, accessed 18 October 2010.
4. "Fastest Growing Churches in America," *Outreach*, Special issue 2010, 41, 43.

Chapter 2 Hopes, Dreams, and Delays

1. John 10:10.
2. Paraphrase of John 3:16.
3. 2 Samuel 12:8, emphasis added.
4. Ephesians 3:20.
5. Isaiah 61:1–3, 6.

Chapter 3 God's Game Plan for Winning at Life

1. Genesis 37:5–9.
2. See John 3.
3. John 15:5.
4. James 1:2–4.
5. Genesis 39:2–4.
6. Proverbs 3:11–12.
7. Genesis 50:19–21.
8. Genesis 39:3.
9. Genesis 39:23.
10. 1 Samuel 17:37.

Chapter 4 Parables, Baseball, and the Home Run Life

1. John C. Maxwell, *The 21 Indispensable Qualities of a Leader* (Nashville: Thomas Nelson, 1999), 4, 6.
2. Matthew 22:37–39.
3. Colossians 3:23–24.
4. Matthew 28:19–20.
5. 1 John 4:20.

Chapter 5 Home Plate: How to Win with God

1. Frederick Buechner, *The Magnificent Defeat* (New York: Harper One, 1966), 13.
2. Genesis 25:23.
3. Genesis 28:13–15.
4. Genesis 28:20–21.
5. Genesis 27:19.
6. Frederick Buechner, *The Magnificent Defeat*, 18.
7. Ecclesiastes 2:26.
8. Romans 7:15, 18–19.
9. Matthew 7:7.
10. James 4:8.
11. John 15:1–17.
12. John 14:23–24.
13. John 15:1–17.
14. Matthew 22:37–40.
15. Matthew 28:18–20.
16. John 15:5.
17. Joseph M. Scriven, "What a Friend We Have in Jesus."
18. John 15:5, emphasis added.

Chapter 6 First Base: How to Win Within

1. Barry Newman, "This Town Is Going Down, and Strawberries Share the Blame," *Wall Street Journal*, 19 April 2010, http://online.wsj.com/article/SB10001424052702304172404575169014291111050.html?KEYWORDS=sinkhole, accessed 14 March 2011.
2. Judges 13:3–5.
3. Judges 13:24–25.
4. Deuteronomy 7:1–4.
5. Joshua 23:12–13.
6. Judges 14:2, 3.
7. Numbers 6:1–8.

8. Judges 15:15.
9. 1 Corinthians 5:12–13.
10. 1 Corinthians 6:9–11.
11. Malachi 3:6–12.
12. Ephesians 4:31.
13. 1 John 2:1–2.

Chapter 7 Second Base: How to Win with Others

1. Genesis 25:29–34.
2. Genesis 27.
3. Genesis 34:13.
4. Genesis 38:18.
5. Genesis 34:25.
6. Genesis 37:34–35.
7. Genesis 42:22.
8. Genesis 42:36, 38.
9. Genesis 45:4–8.

Chapter 8 Third Base: How to Win Results

1. Genesis 1:1.
2. Genesis 41:40
3. Judges 20:16.
4. 1 Samuel 17:34–35.
5. Matthew 25:15.
6. Luke: 19:11–27.
7. Mark 10:37.

Chapter 9 Scoring: How to Keep Living and Winning God's Way

1. James 4:3.
2. Ecclesiastes 1:14.
3. Ecclesiastes 12:12–14, The Message.
4. Luke 12:15.
5. Matthew 6:19–21.
6. Matthew 16:26.
7. 2 Peter 3:10–12.
8. Philippians 2:9–11.
9. Romans 11:36.
10. 1 Corinthians 10:31.
11. Colossians 3:23–24.
12. 1 Corinthians 10:31.

13. Genesis 50:19–21.
14. Matthew 20:26–28.
15. John 3:16.
16. Stephen King, Commencement Address, Vassar College, May 20, 2001, http://commencement.vassar.edu/2001/010520.king.html, accessed March 7, 2013.